Screen Shots

Creating your own Web site

with FrontPage Express

Creating your own Web site

with FrontPage Express

Patrick BEUZIT

First published in the United Kingdom in 2001 by Hachette UK

© English Translation Hachette UK 2001
© Hachette Livre: Marabout Informatique 2000

English translation by Prose Unlimited

Concept and editorial direction: Ghéorghiï Vladimirovitch Grigorieff (grigorieff@imaginet.be)

Additional research and editorial assistance: Simon Woolf, Rod Cuff, John Cardinal.

A CIP catalogue for this book is available from the British Library

Trademarks/Registered Trademarks

ISBN: 1 84202 042 0

Designed by Graph'M
Layout by Nicolas Thomisse
Typeset in Humanist 521
Printed and bound by Graficas Estella, Spain

Hachette UK
Cassell & Co
The Orion Publishing Group
Wellington House
London
WC2R 0BB

Web site: www.marabout.com/Cassell

Contents

CONTENTS

Chapter 1

Introduction

What is a Web site?

A Web site is a set of documents (text, images, sound, video etc.) placed on and accessible via the Internet and grouped into one or more pages. The purpose of the site is to provide information to Internet **users**. So, for example, a trading company may showcase its products and core activity, and offer goods for sale, whilst a private individual may wish to discuss his or her hobbies, or feature friends and family … It's all about grabbing your fifteen seconds of fame. Your imagination is the only limit! To get an idea of just what an incredible creation the Web is and exactly how much information is out there waiting for you, just try browsing for a few hours. The sites that you uncover in that time will just be the tip of the iceberg.

T he smallest sites consist of just a single page, but most sites have several, or indeed, many pages. These pages are text files or documents that can be viewed with any word processor. The documents are composed of commands written in **HTML** (Hyper Text Markup Language) which is a description language used to format the text (i.e. to define the size, colour, appearance, location in the page etc.) and the images (their size, location in relation to text etc.).

A ll the pages are interlinked by hypertext links. A hypertext link is a word, a set of words or an image on which you click with the mouse to access a second page, or a different part of the current page. You can thus "click" through all the pages of the site one after the other. The concept of the Web is based on hypertext technology.

T oday, creating a Web site is the best possible way to publish your own information. A Web site is accessible everywhere in the world. It has never been easier to reach such a wide audience. All it takes is a little effort to format and present your site – and remember, I have a Web site, therefore I am!

Structure of a Web site

Take a closer look at the Mirabilis Web site:

http://www.mirabilis.com

The (visible) tip of the iceberg...

The hidden mass...

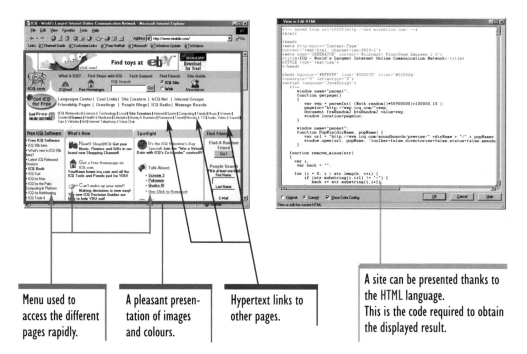

Do you have to be an HTML whiz to create your own Web site? Do you have to master this complicated, indigestible formal language? Not at all! Luckily, there are excellent editors available which you can use to create a Web site without knowing anything of HTML.

Menu used to access the different pages rapidly.

A pleasant presentation of images and colours.

Hypertext links to other pages.

A site can be presented thanks to the HTML language.
This is the code required to obtain the displayed result.

Unlike a Microsoft Word document, a Web site is not a single file comprising several pages, images, video and audio files etc. There will be as many HTML files as there are pages on the site. However, images are not saved in these files, but are independent documents.

Briefly

A Web site is constructed in three main steps

❶ Development

This is probably the longest step, though not necessarily the most complex. Originality and a certain artistic sense are a distinct advantage here. The most difficult part is determining how many pages your site will contain, how they will be structured and accessed and what kind of information they will provide to users. Once this has all been decided, your work will consist of formatting the text and images.

❷ Publication on the Internet

Keeping your masterpiece on your hard disk is not such a good idea, as no one will be able to access it. So you'll have to find a place on the Internet for it. The most suitable solution would be to use the resources of an ISP (Internet Service Provider), provided that they include this service in their package. Otherwise, there are numerous servers that will accommodate your Web site free of charge. You'll find that you can publish your Web site in a matter of minutes.

❸ Registration with search engines

For your site to get noticed and become popular with users, you therefore need to get it listed with a search engine or two. This step is optional, but a site that is not properly referenced has little chance of being visited. The Web is so immense that your site will be as one minute speck of plankton floating in a whole ocean of the stuff.

The Tools

To create a Web site, you will need a Web site editor. And you need not invest in complex and expensive HTML editors when Windows 98 offers a simple and efficient application for that purpose called Microsoft FrontPage Express, which is not only simple, but also free! As you become more proficient in developing Web sites, you may need to use a more robust tool such as Microsoft FrontPage 2000, the professional version for which you have to pay.

A Web site can also feature attractive visual effects such as images, photographs, buttons etc. You will therefore also need a drawing tool. Paint Shop Pro may be just what you need, as it is powerful yet relatively simple to use. What is more, you can download it from http://www.jasc.com and try it, free of charge, for 30 days (more than enough time to create your Web site). An alternative to Paint Shop Pro is Microsoft Paint, which is delivered as a standard with Windows 95 and 98. Basic but more than sufficient to create small images, Microsoft Paint can be installed on all Windows platforms (Microsoft Paint is accessible from Start/Programs/Paint).

Curious? Then try one of the following HTML editors, no less professional and just as recommendable:	
Dreamweaver http://www.macromedia.com	Dreamweaver is the ideal solution for the design and creation of Websites with a professional touch.
Home Page http://www.filemaker.com	Tool allowing the creation of Web pages without requiring any knowledge of HTML on the part of the user. Powerful, yet simple, it is meant for beginners as well as for professionals.
FrontPage 2000 http://www.microsoft.com	Microsoft FrontPage 2000 is a comprehensive product (see page 14).
Netscape Composer http://home.netscape.com	A tool meant for beginners, its advantage being that it is free, since it is included with Netcape Communicator.
ColdFusion http://www.allaire.com	A suite of integrated tools for creating your own business on the Internet. These tools can be used to create ordinary and e-commerce Web sites.

Installing FrontPage Express

Microsoft FrontPage Express is delivered with Windows 98. Make sure that it has been installed on your PC.

① Click Start, then Settings, Control Panel, and then Add/Remove Programs.

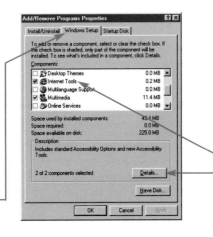

② Click Windows Setup.

③ Select Internet Tools and click Details.

④ Make sure that Microsoft FrontPage Express is ticked. If not, tick it and then click OK to confirm.

⑤ You will be asked to insert the Windows 98 CD-ROM.

Microsoft FrontPage Express is not integrated into Windows 95. It is however delivered with Internet Explorer Version 4.0 or higher (full installation). It is highly likely in fact that, unbeknownst to you, FrontPage Express is already installed on your hard disk!

FrontPage 2000's major features:

FrontPage 2000 includes features that help in the creation of Web pages.

Features designed to help in the creation of Web pages.

- **Customised themes.**
- **Pixel-resolution positioning and use of layers (a technique that allows superimposition of objects).**
- **DHTML animations.**
- **Colour-management tools.**
- **Cascading style sheets (CSS).**

Use of the HTML language made easy.

- **Insertion of codes using buttons or pull-down menus.**
- **Preservation of HTML code, especially the order of tags and remarks, upper- and lower-case and spaces.**
- **Customisation of HTML formatting.**
- **Display of HTML tags in a WYSIWYG (= What You See Is What You Get) view.**

Integration of databases.

Database Request Assistant (easy incorporation of database requests into your pages).
A "Create database" button allows creation or modification of an Access database. This operation is as easy as creating a form.

Accommodates the latest Web technologies.

- **Webbot components.**
- **Microsoft Script Editor. This integrated editor simplifies the modification and debugging of scripts, specially JavaScript and Microsoft Visual Basic Scripting Edition.**
- **Editing of HTML, DHTML, script, ASP and XML formats.**
The HTML tag allows the display and modification of pages and scripts, especially those with HTML, DHTML, script, ASP (Active Server Pages) and XML (Extensible Markup Language) formats.

Expansion and programming possibilities.

- **Microsoft Visual Basic for Applications.**
- **Models of applications, documents and Web objects.**
These models allow the developer to manipulate FrontPage and Web pages by the use of programming.
- **Extending the features of FrontPage using the Web Microsoft Visual InterDev development system.**

Chapter 2

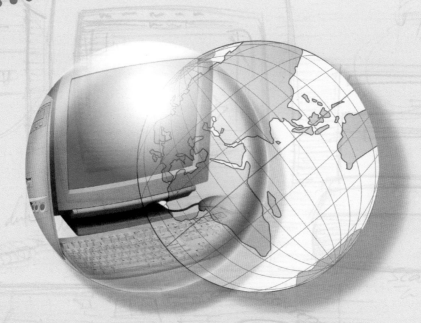

Microsoft FrontPage Express

Starting FrontPage Express

Check list

To start *Microsoft Front-Page Express*, click *Start*, then *Programs*, then *Internet Tools*. Now find *FrontPage Express*.
Explore the other folders if you're interested.

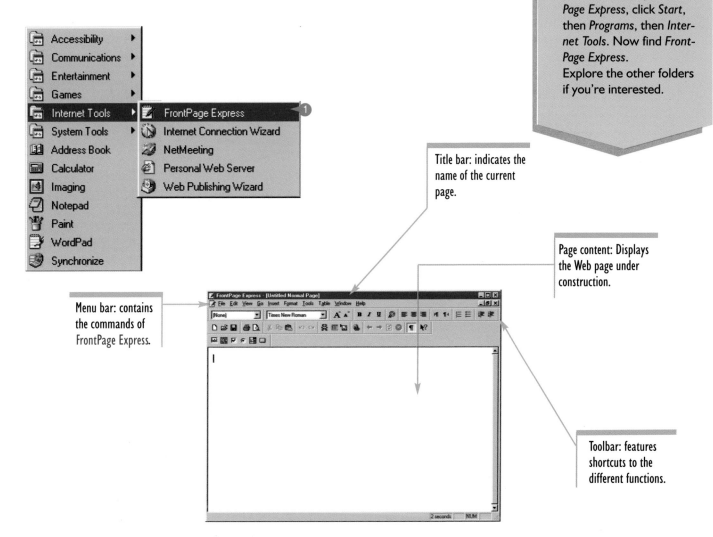

Title bar: indicates the name of the current page.

Page content: Displays the Web page under construction.

Menu bar: contains the commands of FrontPage Express.

Toolbar: features shortcuts to the different functions.

Configuring Microsoft FrontPage Express

Step 1: Click the *View* menu and make sure all the tool-bars are ticked.

✔ Standard Toolbar
✔ Format Toolbar
✔ Forms Toolbar
✔ Status Bar
✔ Format Marks

Refresh
HTML...

Step 2 The *Go* menu is used to start the *e-mail address book* and the *News reader*.

Similarly, the *Internet Call* menu is used to run *Netmeeting*, the videoconferencing software.

This menu is not essential to know about when you're constructing a Web site...

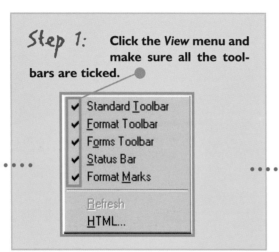

Step 3 Finally, go to *Tools / Font Options*, and make sure that "US/ Western European" are the default fonts.

Font Options

If you create web pages in different languages you can set the default fonts to use with each character set.

Character set:

Korean
Multilingual (UTF-8)
Simplified Chinese (GB2312)
Thai
Traditional Chinese (Big5)
Turkish
US/Western European
Vietnamese

Proportional font: Times New Roman
Fixed-width font: Courier New
MIME encoding: iso-8859-1

OK   Cancel   Help

Creating a folder under Windows in three easy steps

Before you get down to work, you should create a folder on your hard disk to contain your Web site. This is where you will save all the pages, images and other files of your site.

The *My Documents* folder seems ideally suited for this purpose, so you should create a new subfolder called "Web" in it: *C:\My Documents\Web.*

1 Start Windows Explorer and select the folder (directory) in which you wish to create a new subfolder.

2 Click File, New and then Folder.

3 Now enter the name of the subfolder you wish to create.

C:\My Documents\Web becomes your working folder.

The images which will grace your site must also be copied to your working folder. You can, if you prefer, create yet another subfolder called "Images", for example, to contain all the images of your site:

C:\My Documents\Web\ Images.

Creating subdirectories (subfolders) may not necessarily be the best way to proceed. Once you have finished your site, you'll want to publish it on the Internet, i.e. find a service that will host it free of charge. And some such services do not allow the use of subdirectories! In other words, all the files of your Web site will have to be in a single directory. You will run into this problem if your ISP is CompuServe, for example. Nevertheless, this restriction is relatively rare, and we suggest that you store your images in C:\My Documents\Web\Images.

If you intend to feature sound on your Web site, you should create a sound subdirectory, e.g. C:\My Documents\Web\Sound.

Once you have defined the structure of your Web page, you must gather all the documents you need to construct it. Photographs, images and clipart will liven up your site. Consider the editorial line, the way the information will be presented, how to navigate through the site, etc. The ideal solution is to create a storyboard that shows the different pages you want to develop and that specifies the contents of each.

Baie Orientale, Long Bay, Oyster Pond, Anse de Grande Saline... fabulous, sun-drenched, sandy beaches, with limpid blue waters, the lapping of the waves, the fragrance of the bracing brine-soaked wind... a symphony for the senses that begs you to sit back and enjoy it.

"Saint-Martin - Saint-Barthélemy" - Tourist Guide from Plein Sud - Ulysse publishers.

In this book, we'll create a tourism Web site about the island of Saint-Martin, which is situated in the Caribbean, to the north of Guadaloupe. This site will present the island, its beaches, inhabitants, customs etc.

When you have gone through this book, you'll be able to create your own Web site and bring it to the notice of thousands of users logged on throughout the world.

You can find the Web site at: http://www.multimania.com/sxm/
And download it from: http://www.multimania.com/sxm/site.zip

Chapter 3

Basic operations

Creating a new page

Creating a page does not pose any particular problems. You must simply remember to save your page immediately after creating it. Furthermore, you will find it useful to prepare all the pages in advance. So you should have a precise idea of how your Web site will be structured and how many pages it will contain.

New Page

Template or Wizard:

Normal Page
Confirmation Form
Form Page Wizard
New Web View Folder
Personal Home Page Wizard
Survey Form

OK
Cancel
Help

Description

Create a blank web page.

1 Click File, then New. Select Normal Page.

2 Now click File, then Page Properties.

3 Give your document a title. This title will appear in the title bar of the user's browser. Avoid accents, because some search engines that use the title to reference sites tend to ignore accented characters, so your site may not be properly referenced as a result.

4 Leave the Base Location field empty.

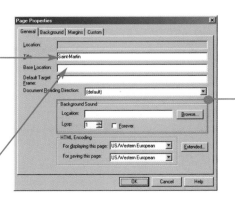

Page Properties

General | Background | Margins | Custom |

Location:
Title: Saint-Martin
Base Location:
Default Target Frame:
Document Reading Direction: [default]

Background Sound
Location: .... Browse...
Loop: 1 ☐ Forever

HTML Encoding
For displaying this page: US/Western European Extended...
For saving this page: US/Western European

OK Cancel Help

TIP

The option Background Sound is used by some browsers to play music when the page is opened. If you want to use background music, however, you need to save the page you have just created first, then go back to Page Properties and now click the Browse button to add the file. The reason for this is explained on page 26. We will come back to background music in Chapter 6.

Modifying its properties

① Click the Background tab to choose the background colour of your page. You may prefer a background image to a plain colour, but you must first save the page, then go back to Properties, and this time select the image file.

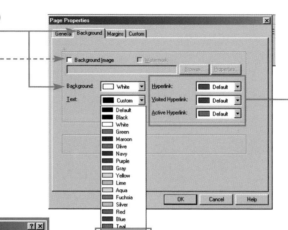

② You can also choose the colour of the hyperlinks, the visited hyperlinks and the active hyperlinks.

③ Select Custom to access a wide range of colours.

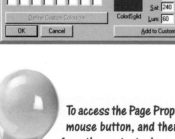

To access the Page Properties, click with the right mouse button, and then select Page Properties from the contextual menu.

Note: You can also access the Background tab presented here by clicking Format / Background.

You're creating your first page. Although it is blank and contains no text or graphics, you should save it immediately on your hard disk.

Saving a page

A newly created page must be saved rapidly to avoid losing it in case of a power outage or if the computer crashes. You should therefore get into the habit of saving your work regularly. Click *File* and then *Save As*.

The page title is displayed automatically.

If you've not created a title yet, enter one now.

The field "Page Location" corresponds to the URL of your Web site. But you may not necessarily know in advance the address of the server that will host your site. So delete what appears in this field.

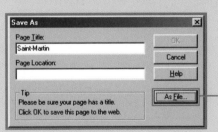

The "OK" button will change to grey, which means that you cannot save the file directly to the Internet.

● Click "As File" to save the file on your hard disk.

Select the folder that will contain all the files of your site. In this example: C:\My Documents\Web.

Call the home page of your Web site "index.htm". Most browsers will look for a page with this name if the user types in a URL (Web address) that does not specify a full file name. Use the extension .htm rather than .html.

Finally, your file names should not exceed eight characters and you must avoid using the space character or special characters such as (, &, ~, #, {, [,], }, @, etc.

Note: A URL (Uniform Resource Locator) is the address of a Web Site. For example:

http://www.marabout. com/cassell

CHAPTER 3 : BASIC OPERATIONS

25

Saving a page (continued)

Your page will now appear on the screen...

● The file name is shown in the title bar.

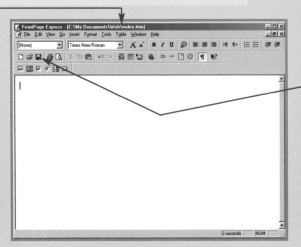

● Now that the page has been saved, you can add a background image rather than a plain colour.

● From now on, you can press the disk icon to save your changes as you work.

● Similarly, if you want music played when your page is loaded, click File, then Page Properties, and specify the audio file you wish to use, or select Insert / Background Sound.

Relative and absolute access path:

Why do you have to save the page and only then add a background image or sound?

Because in this way, the access path to the image file is relative, not absolute. Suppose that the background image, called backgd.gif here, is in the directory C:\My Documents\Web\Images, and that the page is saved in the directory C:\My Documents\Web. The access path to the file will then be entered as Images/backgd.gif.

Now if the page had not been saved at least once, the access path to the file would have been C:\My Documents\Web\Images\backgd.gif. And once the Web site was published on the Internet, browsers would not be able to find any image at this location, simply because there is no such directory as C:\My Documents on the server that hosts your site.

Click File/ Save All to save all documents currently opened in Microsoft FrontPage Express.

Checklist

1. You can open several documents simultaneously in *FrontPage Express*.

2. You can then use the *Cascade* and *Tile* functions to organise the windows you have opened in *FrontPage Express*.

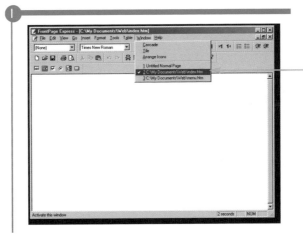

The Window menu is used to switch from one window to the other.

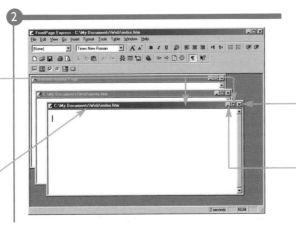

Double click the title bar or the Restore icon of one of the windows for full screen display.

The file access path is shown in the title bar of the page.

Use the Close icon to close the active window rapidly. A dialogue box will ask you whether you wish to save your changes before you close.

Click the Minimize icon to minimise the active window to an icon.

Opening and closing a page

File / Open	File / Close

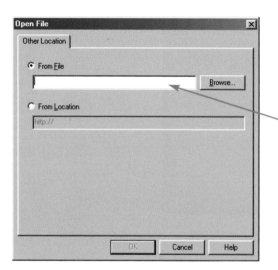

1 Click File, then Open. Use From File to open a page stored on the hard disk. To open a page from the Web, enter its address in the From Location field.

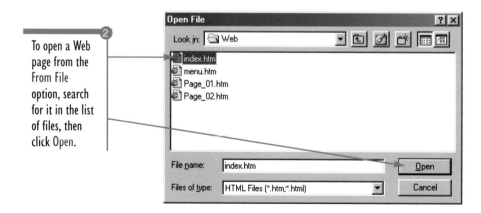

To open a Web page from the From File option, search for it in the list of files, then click Open.

You can close a page you are using, without closing *FrontPage Express*. If you made changes since the last save, the program will ask you whether you wish to save them.

A Web page is constructed in several steps, so you must remember the name you gave to a page under construction so that you can find it easily and continue working on it. You open a saved page in the same way as for any other file saved under Windows.

Opening external Web pages

① Click File, then Open and select the second option. Enter the complete address of the page you wish to retrieve.

In FrontPage Express you can also open a page from an external site and download images from the page retrieved.

② FrontPage Express loads the page and the images.

③ Click View / HTML to view the commands that were used to create this page.

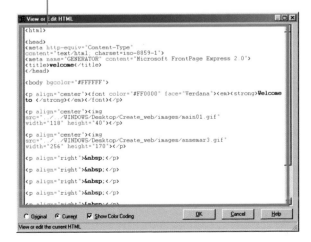

When you save the page, the *HTML* editor suggests that you copy the images of the site on to your hard disk.

This is an easy way to build up a database of images or to study the structure of competing yet friendly Web sites!

Most sites have been created with software other than FrontPage Express. They use features that may not be recognised by the latter. Also, some sites use the latest technologies, such as ASP and PHP, which are server-side scripts. The pages are created dynamically, in real time. It is therefore not possible for FrontPage to retrieve them because they do not even exist!

Testing your Site

It's not easy to guarantee that a finished site will look the way it is supposed to look. Although *FrontPage Express* is an *HTML* editor that displays the page as it will be seen in the browser, there is nothing like a full-size test. We are at times surprised by formatting differences from one browser to another. This is especially true when a user has a hardware configuration different from yours.

So you should test your site regularly with your favourite browser. Even better, you should use several browsers to test the site, ideally *Microsoft Internet Explorer* and *Netscape Communicator*, so that you can gauge the differences between them.

It would be rather difficult to test our Web site on tourism in Saint-Martin, since we've only just started creating it. For our example, we will use Netscape to view another site stored on the hard disk:

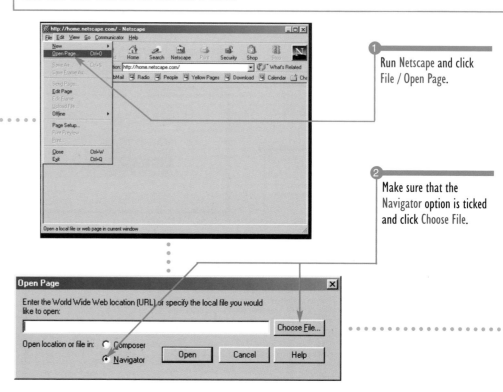

Run Netscape and click File / Open Page.

Make sure that the Navigator option is ticked and click Choose File.

Testing your Site (continued)

To view a Web page using Internet Explorer, click File / Browse then search for the name of the file on the hard disk. To refresh a page, press the Refresh button.

③ Search your hard disk for the Web page you want to view. A Web page file ends with .htm or .html.

Select the file, and click Open.

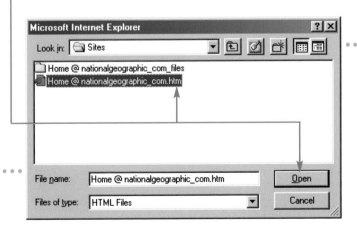

④ The site appears in the browser. There is no point connecting to the Internet to see what a Web site stored on your hard disk looks like.

TIP

When you make changes in your Web pages in Microsoft FrontPage Express, make sure you always save the page concerned. You can then view the result in your browser, but you should press the Reload button, because otherwise the changes may not necessarily appear. You might get the impression that your changes were not entered correctly, whereas what has really happened is that the browser has not taken them into account.

Chapter 4

The text

Inserting text

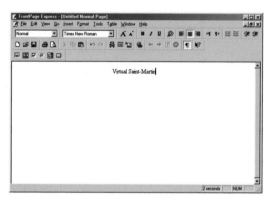

Inserting text in Microsoft FrontPage Express could not be simpler. You simply type words in the main window as in a word processor.

Text is the basic element of an Internet site. A site consisting only of images would take too long to load; one consisting only of text would be boring to read. The ideal solution is to strike the right balance between the two.

You can use the toolbar to format your text quickly and easily:

Change style.

Change font.

Text colour.

Align Right / Centre / Align Left.

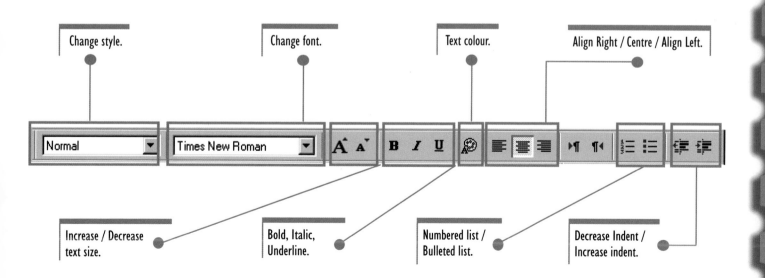

Increase / Decrease text size.

Bold, Italic, Underline.

Numbered list / Bulleted list.

Decrease Indent / Increase indent.

The Enter key

You must pay particular attention to the Enter key.

Use it on its own to start a new paragraph, and *Shift+Enter* to start a new line in the same paragraph.

The difference is subtle, but visible.

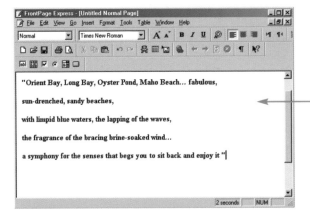

1 When you press Enter, each line is actually a new paragraph. So this text consists of five paragraphs.

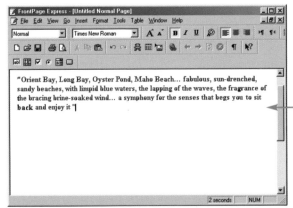

2 When you press Shift+Enter, you start a new line. This text consists of a single paragraph.

3 The Shift key is often represented by an up arrow on the keyboard.

The spacing between two paragraphs is much larger than the spacing between two lines of the same paragraph.

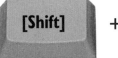

[Shift] + **[Enter]**

Formatting your text

Format / Font

Edit / Font Properties

Your PC probably has an impressive number of fonts. If any font that you specify in your Web page is not installed on the PC of the user who visits your site, it will be replaced by an equivalent font. The site may then look different from what you would expect, because when different fonts are used, the formatting is distorted. So you should avoid using exotic fonts, and stick to widely used standards such as *Arial*, *Courier New*, *Times New Roman*, *Symbol* or *Verdana*, for example.

Select the text you want to format, using the mouse, then click Format/Font.

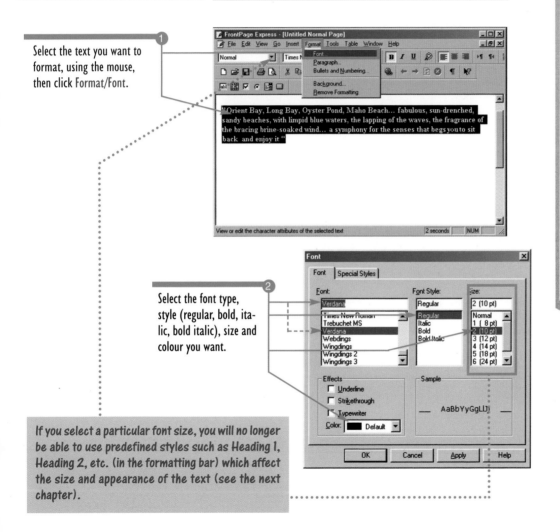

Select the font type, style (regular, bold, italic, bold italic), size and colour you want.

If you select a particular font size, you will no longer be able to use predefined styles such as Heading 1, Heading 2, etc. (in the formatting bar) which affect the size and appearance of the text (see the next chapter).

Click the *Special Styles* tab and tick the options you want. Special styles such as *Citation*, *Sample*, *Definition*, *Code*, *Variable*, etc. are predefined in *HTML*.

The Citation style is used for citations, literary texts, etc.

The Blink style makes your text blink, and should be used in moderation, if at all.

The Bold and Italic styles can be selected through either the Font or the Special Styles tab. You should use the latter.

Vertical position is used to display text as subscript or superscript.

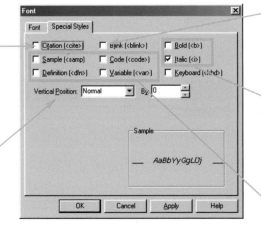

The Sample, Code, Definition and Variable styles are used frequently to display technical documents or samples.

The Remove formatting option is used to return to plain text.

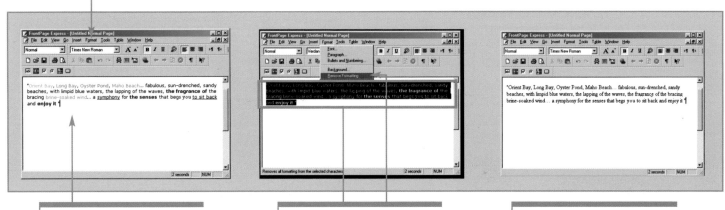

In this example, the text is in different colours, with some words in bold, others in italic, etc.

Select the text, then go to the Format menu and click Remove formatting.

The text will be displayed again in Times New Roman, in black, and normal size.

Predefined styles

Format / Paragraph

Predefined styles are used to format headings, paragraphs or addresses quickly and easily.

Microsoft FrontPage Express features a set of predefined styles. They are applied to entire paragraphs and not to a portion of text only.

The styles can be accessed through the Microsoft FrontPage toolbar or through Format/Paragraph.

Normal ▼

Address
Bulleted List
Defined Term
Definition
Directory List
Formatted
Heading 1
Heading 2
Heading 3
Heading 4
Heading 5
Heading 6
Menu List
Normal
Numbered List

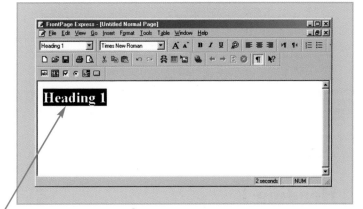

1 Place the cursor on the paragraph you wish to format, or select the paragraph with the mouse.

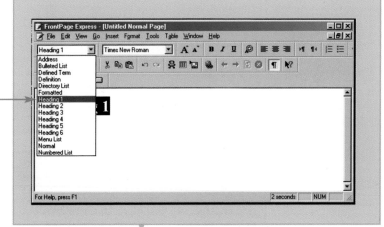

2 Click Heading I.

Predefined styles (continued)

However, the text may remain unchanged, even though you selected and applied a style.

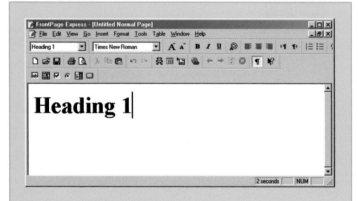

The paragraph is automatically formatted according to the Heading 1 style.

The font size was forced to 2. The formatting takes priority over predefined styles, and this explains why the text did not change. All you have to do to correct this is to remove the formatting of the text (Format/Remove formatting) and apply the Heading 1 style again.

④ Create a line of text with the font Verdana, font size 2 and in bold.

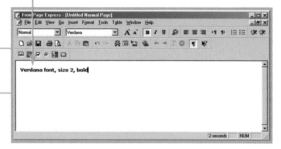

⑤ Select the line and apply Heading 1.

⑥ The line remains unchanged, even though Heading 1 appears in the style bar.

Here are the main predefined styles

Predefined styles in HTML are not comparable to styles in Microsoft Word. HTML provides only basic styles that you modify. For instance, the formatting of two lines with the same Heading 1 style may be very different if you specify a particular colour or font for each of the two lines. So predefined styles cannot be used for uniform formatting. As a prospective Webmaster, you must therefore be very careful about the text characteristics (font size, colour, etc.) in your pages. Otherwise, you will have to use style sheets, a more advanced mechanism whose description lies beyond the scope of this book.

All things considered, predefined styles are of limited value, but they are nonetheless worth a try.

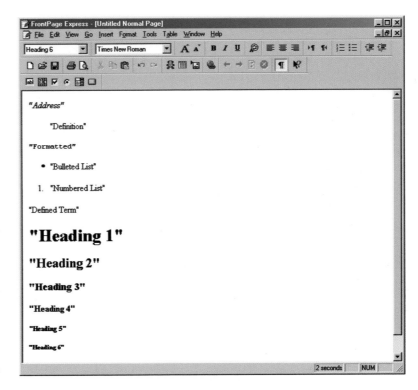

A Webmaster is a person who creates and maintains a Web site.

Importing text

Insert /File

As its name implies, the import text function (accessible via *Insert/File*) is used to import documents created using another application, such as a word processor. This function is very useful because it saves you the trouble of having to type in text. In theory, you can import *Word*, *WordPerfect*, *Excel* and other such files, but you should bear in mind that formatted text is not always imported properly. So you should limit yourself to importing plain text.

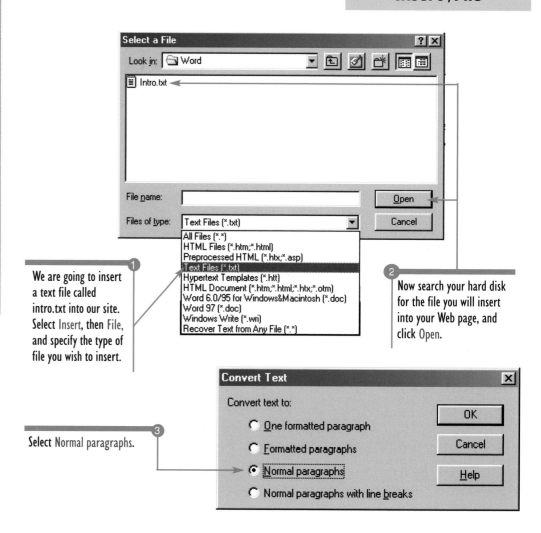

We are going to insert a text file called intro.txt into our site. Select Insert, then File, and specify the type of file you wish to insert.

Now search your hard disk for the file you will insert into your Web page, and click Open.

Select Normal paragraphs.

Formatting

Use the mouse to select the text just inserted into the Web page, and change the font type, size and colour, if necessary.

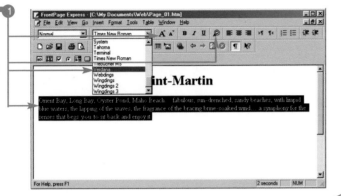

When the window size of FrontPage Express is changed, the text extends to fit the page width, but does not necessarily change in appearance.

Change the indentation with forced new-lines. Remember: you must press Shift + Enter for a new line.

New-line markers appear on the screen when you click the Show/Hide icon. These visible markers will help you check the formatting, but will not be visible through the browser once you have finished the site.

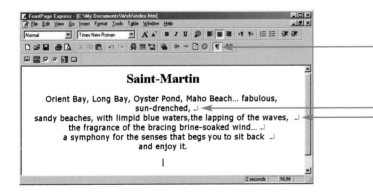

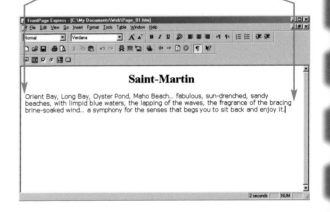

New-line characters are generated by pressing Shift + Enter.

Importing documents

For some obscure reason, it is not possible to import documents created with *Word 97*.

Import text created with Microsoft Word. Then click Open.

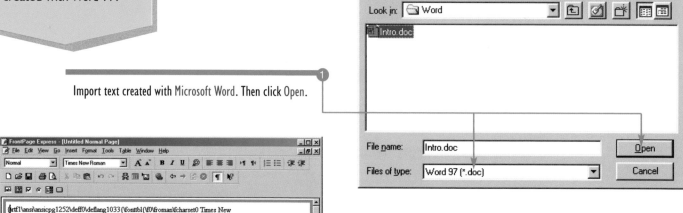

The imported text contains illegible control codes. Removing them manually would be a tedious task. So you should limit your use of the Import function just to text-only files, created with Windows Notepad, for example.

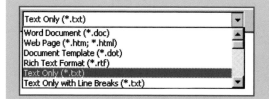

If you absolutely have to insert a document created with Word 97 into your Web site, then you must save it as "Text Only".

Horizontal lines

Insert / Horizontal Line

With *FrontPage Express* you can add horizontal lines to a Web site, and then change their length and thickness as you wish. These lines are very useful for separating the different sections of a Web page.

1 Place the cursor at the place where you wish to insert a horizontal line and click Insert/Horizontal Line.

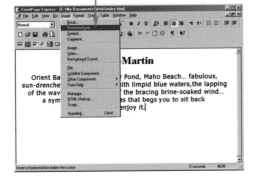

2 The line will span the entire width of the FrontPage Express window. Double click on the horizontal line to modify its properties.

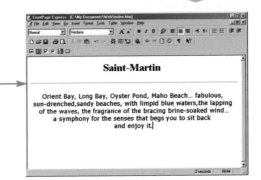

3 Enter a smaller width, for example 70 percent of the window. Change the line height and colour if necessary, and click OK.

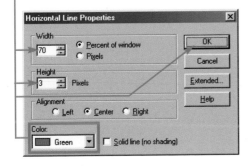

4 The line width and colour have changed. To delete the horizontal line, select it, then press Delete on the keyboard.

Insert / Symbol

Inserting special characters into a Web page is very easy. Select the Insert menu and click *Symbol*.

Place the cursor at the point where you wish to insert a symbol. In this example, you will insert quotation marks.

Select the symbol you want from the list, and click Insert.

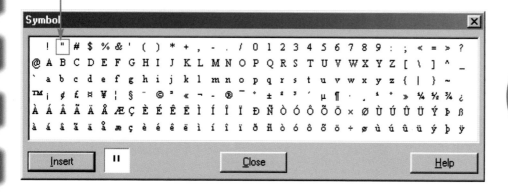

Tip

Some browsers may not be able to display the symbols in this list correctly. So you should use them sparingly.

Chapter 5

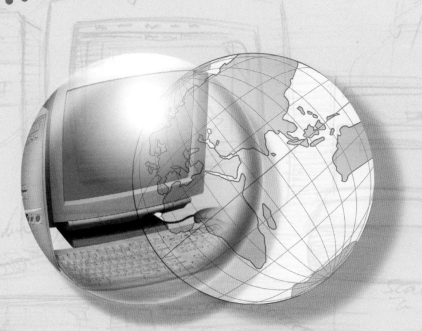

Graphics

Introduction

As a Webmaster, you must always bear in mind that your site will be visited by people with hardware configurations very different from yours. Some use slow modems, others access the Internet via cable or special lines. You must therefore make sure that the site does not take too long to load, because visitors, not known for their patience, might decide to give up.

You must therefore pay particular attention to the size of the images you use. Similarly, you must avoid using excessively high or wide images, because they might not be fully displayed on computers that do not support high screen resolutions.

When you insert an image into a Word document, it becomes an integral part of the file. When you save the document, you also save the image in one single file.

Inserting an image into a Web page is completely different. When you save the page, the image is not saved, but only the name of the directory and of the file where the image is contained.

If you insert an image into your Web page, and then delete it from the hard disk, the next time you open this page, FrontPage Express will not be able to find the file. For this reason, you must always keep the files you use.

Once you have finished your site, you will place the HTML files and all the images used on the Internet. This set of files constitutes the site proper.

Finally, you should keep all the images in a single directory, as this will make it easier for you to publish your site on the Internet.

The working directory of the site in our example is C:\My Documents\Web. So you should create a directory C:\My Documents\Web\Images to contain the images and logos.

File formats

Name	Size	Type	Modified
map.gif	8KB	ACDSee GIF Image	18/10/99 16:42
menu1.gif	2KB	ACDSee GIF Image	10/09/99 12:57
menu2.gif	2KB	ACDSee GIF Image	10/09/99 12:57
menu3.gif	2KB	ACDSee GIF Image	10/09/99 12:58
menu4.gif	3KB	ACDSee GIF Image	10/09/99 12:58
menu5.gif	3KB	ACDSee GIF Image	17/09/99 10:32
menu6.gif	3KB	ACDSee GIF Image	06/10/99 09:56
orientbay.jpg	15KB	ACDSee JPG Image	10/09/99 12:37
orientbay3.bmp	141KB	ACDSee BMP Image	11/02/00 23:17
title01.jpg	2KB	ACDSee JPG Image	06/10/99 10:11
title02.jpg	3KB	ACDSee JPG Image	23/09/99 12:55
title03.jpg	4KB	ACDSee JPG Image	29/09/99 09:46
title04.jpg	3KB	ACDSee JPG Image	13/10/99 10:04

If you use a format other than GIF or JPG, the image will be automatically converted to GIF, for the simple reason that browsers can recognise only these two formats.

With *Microsoft Front-Page Express* you can insert images from different applications and therefore in different formats.

The format of an image is indicated by the file extension.

The best known image formats are BMP, GIF, JPG, WMF, etc.

So you do not have to worry about the format of the images you use, because they will be automatically converted. Nevertheless, we will show you in Chapter 6 how you can convert images to GIF or JPG format yourself.

The extension of a file, represented by the last three characters, indicates the origin and the format of the document. For example, a file with the extension .doc is very likely to be a Word document; a file with the extension .xls is an Excel file. Files with the extension .htm or .html are Web pages. Finally, files with the extensions .BMP, .GIF, .JPG, .PCX, .PIC, .PNG, .TIF, .WMF, etc. are graphics files.

List of main graphics formats:

BMP	Bitmap graphics format in the Windows environment		PCD	Kodak Photo
CDR	Corel Draw		PCT	Macintosh
DRW	Draw Micrographics		PCX	PaintBrush
GIF	CompuServe		PIC	PCPaint
IFF	Amiga		PNG	Portable Network Graphics
JPG	Jpeg, Jfif		RLE	CompuServe/Windows
LBM	Deluxe Paint		PSD	Photoshop
MAC	MacPaint		TIF	Tagged Image Format
MSP	Microsoft Paint		WMF	Windows Meta File

Insert / Image

Place the cursor at the point where you wish to insert the image, and then click Insert/Image.

The option From Location is used to insert an image from an external Web site.

The option From File is used to select an image from your hard disk.

Select From File and click Browse.

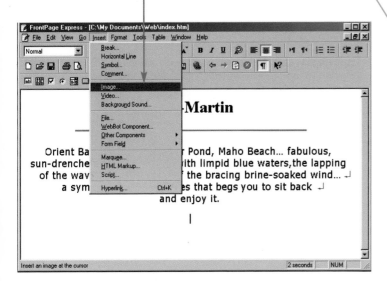

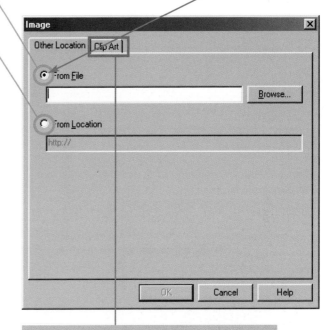

See page 59 on how to insert Clip Art illustrations.

Inserting an image

Find the image you want to insert on your hard disk (usually in **C:\My Documents\Web\ Images**).

In this case, we will insert a photograph of Anse Marcel beach in **BMP** format.

Click Open.

The image appears in the Web page.

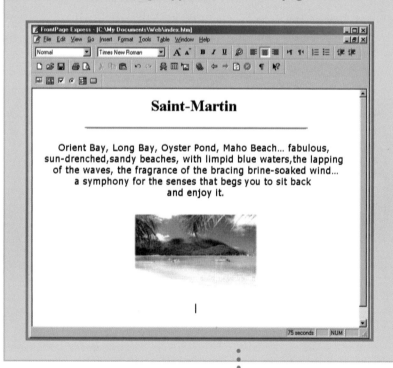

Saving the image

We have seen that *FrontPage Express* can convert images (in other formats) into *GIF* format. The conversion takes place when the Web page is saved.

Save your document immediately after you have inserted the image, by clicking File/Save.

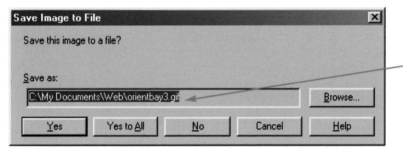

1 FrontPage Express proposes to convert the image you have inserted, which is in BMP format, into GIF format. Remember that the default destination directory proposed by FrontPage Express is C:\My Documents\Web.

2 But we have decided to group the images in the directory C:\My Documents\Web\Images, so we have to change the default path.

3 Now click Yes to confirm the conversion of a BMP image into a GIF image. If you click No, FrontPage Express will ask you the same question the next time you try to save your Web page.

Once the conversion to GIF format has been completed, you can delete or move the initial file in BMP format.

Inserting a "title image"

The title looks dull, so you might wish to insert an image instead.

1 Select the title with the mouse and click on Edit/Clear to delete it.

2 Place the cursor at the point where you wish to insert the image, click Insert/Image and select the file.

When you save the page, FrontPage Express will not suggest converting the image to GIF format, if the image is already in that format.

Edit / Image Properties

You can choose to keep an image in *GIF* format or change it to *JPG* and vice versa in *Image Properties*. This option is used to determine which of the two formats offers the best compression rate, i.e. which generates the smallest file. The best way to find out is to compare the quality and size of the same image.

In general, the *GIF* format is better for logos, clip art or images with high contrast, and the *JPG* format is better for photographic images.

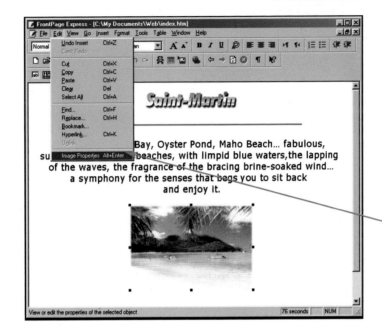

It is important to check and perhaps modify the properties of each image added to the Web site.

Select the first image and click Edit/Image Properties.

The properties of an image can also be accessed by right clicking on the image, by double clicking on the image or by pressing Alt+Enter.

+

You can switch between the two formats used on the Web, i.e. GIF and JPG. When you save the current page, a dialogue box will ask you to convert the image to a specified format (see page 50).

Quality, available only for JPG images, is used to determine the compression rate of the image. The lower the image quality, the higher the compression rate, and therefore the faster the image will load.

The name of the file is given here.

Transparent is used to make the background of an image transparent. We will come back to this notion in Chapter 6.

The Default Hyperlink is used to create a new link. A full chapter is devoted to hyperlinks, so we'll come back to this later.

A Low-Res(olution) image is used to show an approximate picture quickly. The idea is to display an image of mediocre quality which loads very quickly. A visitor to the site is therefore given the impression that the loading has been completed. In fact, the definitive image begins to load when the low resolution image has completed loading.

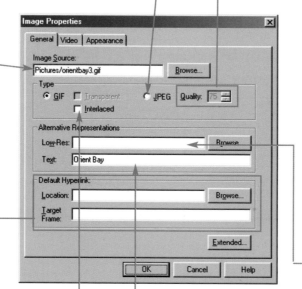

The Interlaced mode, available for GIF images, is used to display the image gradually. The image appears blurred at first, then as it loads it gets gradually sharper and sharper. The visitor gets the feeling of not having to wait so long to see the image.

The Text field is used to enter a comment about the image. This comment is displayed on the Web page as the image is being loaded. Similarly, when you leave the mouse cursor on a image in a browser, the comment is displayed in an information bubble. Finally, some search engines use comments to reference a Web site. So it's a good idea to attach a comment to your images in this way.

Image properties (continued)

The *Video* tab is used to display a video sequence in *.AVI* format. This feature is compatible only with *Internet Explorer*. *Netscape* users will only see the image entered in the *General* tab. So you should avoid using this function.

The Appearance tab is used to adjust the size of the image, specify its position in relation to other elements of the page and add a border.

Horizontal spacing is used to leave a margin to the left and to the right of the image; Vertical spacing for a top and bottom margin.

Border Thickness is used to determine the thickness of the border round the image. A 0 thickness means no border at all.

Finally, Align is used to position the image in relation to other elements (images, text, etc.).

When ticked, Specify Size is used to reduce the size of the displayed image. An image reduced in this way will not however load faster.
To reduce the loading time, you must resize the image using a drawing application.

You can also change the size of an image directly with the mouse. All you have to do is click on one of the four corners of the image and then re-size as you wish.

Image properties (concluded)

Add an informative description to every image. This remark will appear as a tooltip when the user hovers the mouse pointer over the image.

①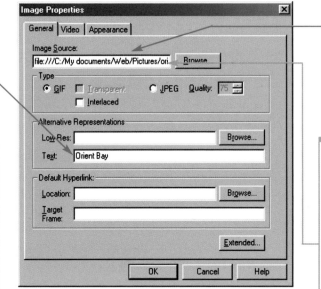

Image Properties

General | Video | Appearance

Image Source:
`file:///C:/My documents/Web/Pictures/ori...` Browse

Type
- ● GIF ☐ Transparent ○ JPEG Quality: 75
- ☐ Interlaced

Alternative Representations
- Low Res: _____ Browse...
- Text: Orient Bay

Default Hyperlink:
- Location: _____ Browse...
- Target Frame: _____

Extended...

OK | Cancel | Help

② Verify carefully what has been entered in the Image Source field.

This situation arises when the Web page has not yet been saved. As Microsoft FrontPage Express does not know in which directory the Web page under construction will be saved, it can only fill out the path-name with a reference to the default directory.

Disaster! In this example, the image source refers to a file on the hard disk. The complete file path is clearly indicated! But once the Web site is placed on the Internet, browsers will not be able to retrieve the image in the directory C:\My Documents\Web\Images, because there is probably no such directory on the server that hosts the site.

The solution therefore is to delete the image that has just been inserted and to save the page (see Chapter 3). You can then reinsert the image. In this way, the access path will be relative, not absolute.

Clip Art

Clip Art is a general name given to images, illustrations, photographs or logos used in particular to embellish a Web site. *Microsoft FrontPage Express* has a function that can be used to manage images stored on your hard disk.

As you develop a site, you will probably to put together a considerable collection of images... and therefore you'll need to set them in some order.

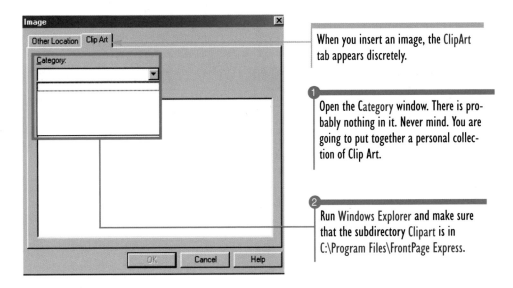

When you insert an image, the ClipArt tab appears discretely.

1 Open the Category window. There is probably nothing in it. Never mind. You are going to put together a personal collection of Clip Art.

2 Run Windows Explorer and make sure that the subdirectory Clipart is in C:\Program Files\FrontPage Express.

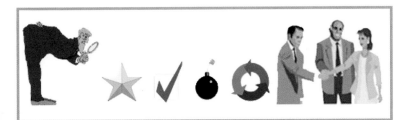

To save an image of a Web site you visit, click on that image with the right mouse button. Select "Save Picture As..", then choose a directory on your hard disk. A copy of the image will then be saved on your PC. After a few hours of browsing, you will have built up a collection of Clip Art, logos and other drawings ready to use.

Clip Art (continued)

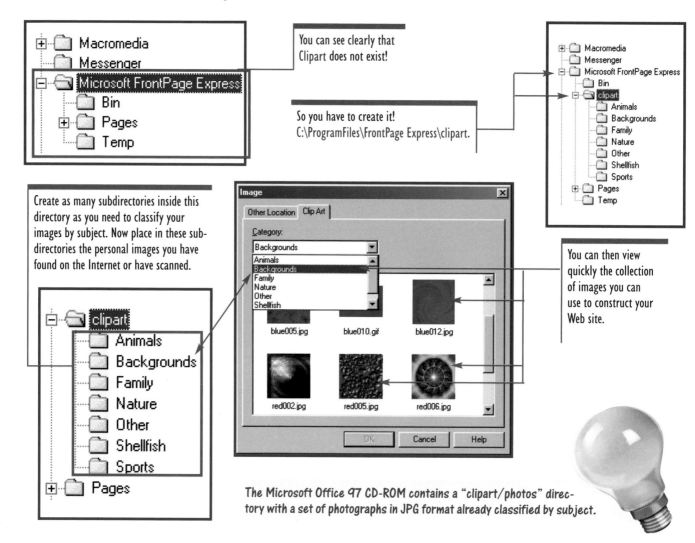

You can see clearly that Clipart does not exist!

So you have to create it!
C:\ProgramFiles\FrontPage Express\clipart.

Create as many subdirectories inside this directory as you need to classify your images by subject. Now place in these subdirectories the personal images you have found on the Internet or have scanned.

You can then view quickly the collection of images you can use to construct your Web site.

The Microsoft Office 97 CD-ROM contains a "clipart/photos" directory with a set of photographs in JPG format already classified by subject.

Copy/Paste

The simplest way to insert an image with *FrontPage Express* is to cut and paste. There is no need to save the image in any format. *FrontPage Express* will do that automatically for you.

1 In Microsoft Paint or another graphics program, open the image you wish to insert in your site. Click Edit/Select All.

2 The image is usually framed by a dotted border.

3 Click Edit/Copy to copy the image.

4 Now go to FrontPage, and paste the image with Edit/Paste.

5 When you save the page, FrontPage Express will suggest you save the image in a file. Click Browse to choose the directory and the name under which the file will be saved.

TIP

The copy/paste function is really very useful for recreating images in GIF format.

CHAPTER 5 : GRAPHICS

61

Web freebies

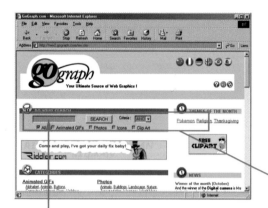

There are sites on the Internet that list numerous free services you as a budding Webmaster may find interesting. Let us take the example of Gograph, a search engine for logos, GIF images, animated images, etc.

1 Select the type of image you want, e.g. animated GIFs, photos, simple icons or clip art. For optimal results, tick All.

2 Now enter a key word and the Gograph search engine will list the different icons found.

These sites are "portals" that will give you access to a treasure trove of really useful information for a Webmaster.

As a Webmaster, you'll need all sorts of tools to construct your site.

These can include applications for drawings, logos or *animated GIF* images (see next chapter), or simply an e-mail address, the name of which announces the purpose of the site (e.g. *saint-martin@ newmail.net*).

Free sites you can ill afford to ignore:

http://freeclutter.snap.com
http://www.allfreestuff.com
http://www.coolfreebies.com
http://www.freesitetools.com
http://www.FreeStuffCentral.com
http://www.freestuffcenter.com
http://www.megafreebies.com
http://www.thefreesite.com
http://www.top20free.com
http://www.freesitex.com

Chapter 6

Tips and techniques

Introduction

Many Web sites are poorly designed. If a site takes too long to load, visitors will move on. If the background images are too dark, the text will not be easy to read. If the images are too large, visitors will have to fiddle constantly with the scroll bars of their browsers. In short, if the content of a site is too bulky and poorly organised, visitors are not likely to venture beyond the homepage. Now, imagine a site that has all these defects and, sad to say, there are a lot of them about.

It is worthwhile therefore to take a look at the different techniques used to construct a Web site that is easy to browse, fast to load and simple to use.

This chapter explains why it is essential to determine the size of your pages in advance.

It also discusses the characteristics of an image and how to convert it into different formats (GIF, JPG, BMP etc.).

The section devoted to the GIF format explains what an animated GIF is and how to create an image with a transparent background.

So, once again, a site must be pleasant to visit and it is up to you, in your new-found role as Webmaster, to make it so. But to spare your potential visitor any extraneous effort and to create a site accessible to all, you will need the right ways and means ... so read on.

Image size

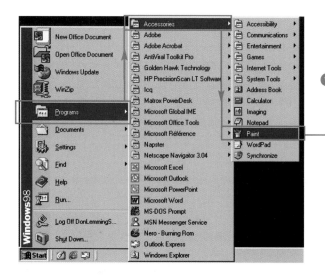

Click Start/Programs/Accessories/Paint to run Microsoft Paint.

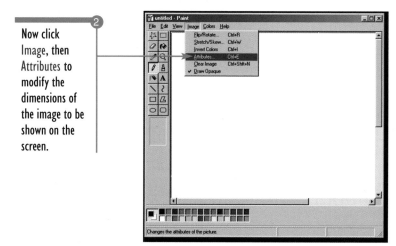

Now click Image, then Attributes to modify the dimensions of the image to be shown on the screen.

Many Net users probably use hardware that differs from yours. For example, the resolution of a graphic display adapter may vary from one PC to another. You must therefore construct a site that can be viewed readily by most users. An image of excessive dimensions cannot be seen in its entirety without using the browser scroll bars, and the site won't be enjoyable to visit.

The dimensions of an image are rarely expressed in centimetres or inches but rather in pixels. A pixel is the smallest point that a computer can display. Let us create an image 200 pixels wide and 150 pixels high with Microsoft Paint.

Creating an image

① Create an image 200 pixels wide and 150 pixels high.

② Remember to tick the Pixels option.

③ In Microsoft Paint, you can also use centimetres as your unit of measure. But as pixels are more widely used, you should get into the habit of dealing in pixels rather than in centimetres.

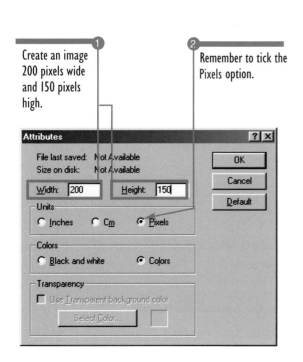

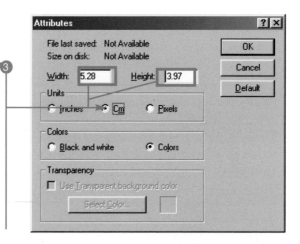

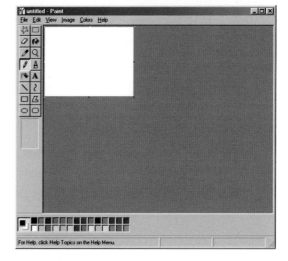

Here is a simple way to create a 200 X 150 pixel image with Microsoft Paint, and to get an idea of the size of such an image.

You are about to unleash your drawing talents....

Hints

There are three categories of PC configuration:

The first category comprises older computers (or rather, older graphic display adapters). They cannot display images larger than 640 X 480 pixels full screen. To view images larger than these, you will have to use your browser's scroll bars.

The second category comprises more powerful adapters, capable of displaying 800 X 600 pixel images.

Finally, the last category comprises recent computers. They can easily display images 1024 pixels wide and 768 pixels high, and even larger.

There is nothing more frustrating than to have to browse a site using the browser's scroll bars. Net surfers are not likely to linger on your pages if they are difficult to read. For this reason, you should adopt one of the following strategies from the outset:

> *The width of images is more important than the height. In fact, using the vertical scroll bars is widely used and accepted. Browsing with horizontal scroll bars, on the other hand, is badly received.*

1. Construct a site that everyone can view easily. Avoid creating images, and by extension a site, more than 640 pixels wide.

   Advantage: Everyone can view the site without having to use the scroll bars.

   Disadvantage: It is not easy to construct a site on a small surface.

2. Construct a site that most visitors can use. The width of the site must not exceed 800 pixels.

   Advantage: The site is easier to format, because you have more working space on which to present text and images.

   Disadvantage: Some, admittedly rare, visitors will have to use their horizontal scroll bars.

3. Construct a high-resolution site.

   Advantage: You can give your imagination free rein and include your every whim and fantasy.

   Disadvantage: Only a very small proportion of visitors will be able to browse your site with pleasure.

   The others will be left out or soon get tired of having to use the scroll bars.

> *Some Webmasters indicate clearly that their site is optimised for 1024 X 768 resolution, for instance. A questionable choice, but the site will be clear and sharp.*

Another method of ensuring that a visitor will see your Web site in the best circumstances is to offer two versions of it: one at 800 x 600 pixels and another at a higher resolution. Nevertheless, maintaining two parallel sites entails twice as much work for the Webmaster!

Artwork

We want to spruce up our Web site on tourism in Saint-Martin by inserting a map of the island. So we searched the Web and found a suitable image for our purpose.

1 Let us first view this image in Microsoft Paint.

2 And then view the image attributes to check its dimensions.

The image is far too large for our site. Visitors will have to use scroll bars to browse it. So we should not use this image.

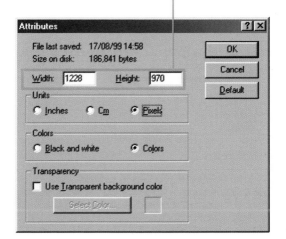

The moral of the story is that, before you fling body and soul into your creative venture, you should determine the size of your pages first. Put yourself in one of the three aforementioned categories and make sure that the dimensions of your site fit perfectly with the characteristics of that category.

Contrary to what many people think, the Internet is not a no-rights zone. Documents on a Web site, whether text or images, cannot be freely used by anyone without permission from their authors and legal owners.

Converting images

Browsers recognise only three formats of graphic images: **GIF**, **JPG** and **PNG**. These three letters represent file extensions. We will not deal with the third format here, as it is still rarely used.

Your site must therefore contain only images in **GIF** or **JPG** format. So if you only have **BMP** images, for instance, you will need to convert them so that they can be used in your site, or let FrontPage Express do it for you!

The **GIF** format (Graphics Interchange Format) is limited to 256 colours. It generates small files, allows transparent backgrounds and can be displayed progressively (first heavily pixellated, then progressively less so until the final image is displayed). As a general rule, we use the **GIF** format for small images, icons or highly-contrasted drawings (text, for example). Later on we shall see the advantages of creating transparent backgrounds.

The **JPG** format uses a lossy compression algorithm. Files saved in this format are not big but there is a loss of quality. Nevertheless, this loss of quality is rarely perceptible to the naked eye.

Knowing how to convert an image can prove very useful, if only to identify the format with the best compression rate. The higher this rate, the faster your Web site will load.

Displaying extensions in Windows Explorer

1 Make sure that the file extensions are displayed in Windows Explorer. In this example, they are not!

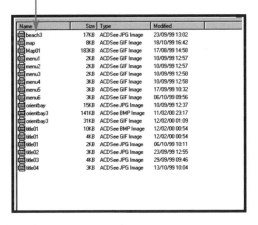

2 In Windows Explorer, click View, then Folder Options.

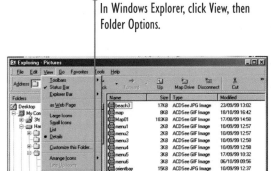

3 Click the View Tab and untick Hide File extensions for known file types.

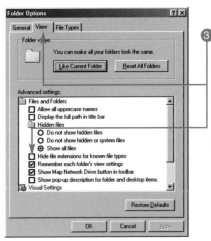

4 The extensions will now appear on the screen.

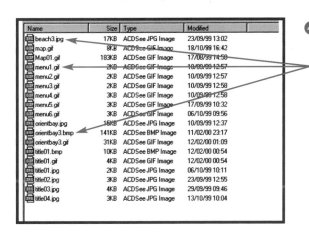

Converting an image

To convert an image, you simply open it in a drawing application and save it in another format. This example shows you how to convert a BMP image into a GIF image in Paint Shop Pro.

Start Paint Shop Pro: Click Start/Programs/Paint Shop Pro then Paint Shop Pro.

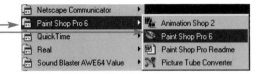

Open the image in Paint Shop Pro. Click File/Open and find the file you want to convert.

Now save it in GIF format. Click File/Save As and select CompuServe Graphics Interchange (GIF).

If you choose GIF, the application will tell you that it has to reduce the number of colours to 256. Click Yes to save the file.

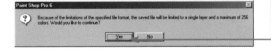

Now run Windows Explorer again and compare the difference in the file sizes of the two images: the GIF format contains an efficient compression algorithm!

Warning: simply renaming a .bmp file to have a .gif extent will not convert it!

Name	Size	Type
ansemar3.bmp	183KB	ACDSee BMP Image
ansemar3.gif	30KB	ACDSee GIF Image

To view the size of files in Windows Explorer, click View then Details.

Image size

The *size* of an image is the storage it occupies on the hard disk. This size is expressed in kilo-bytes. We are not so much concerned with the size in itself, but rather with the time the image takes to load, which necessarily depends on the size of the image file.

That is why you should avoid using excessively large files.

And the size of a file in turn depends not only on the characteristics of that file (dimensions, number of colours) but also on the format in which it is saved (*GIF*, *BMP*, *JPG*, etc.).

Run Windows Explorer and go to the directory that contains your images.

You will see clearly the size of your files, i.e. the amount of space they take up on the hard disk.

The size of an image varies according to the format used.

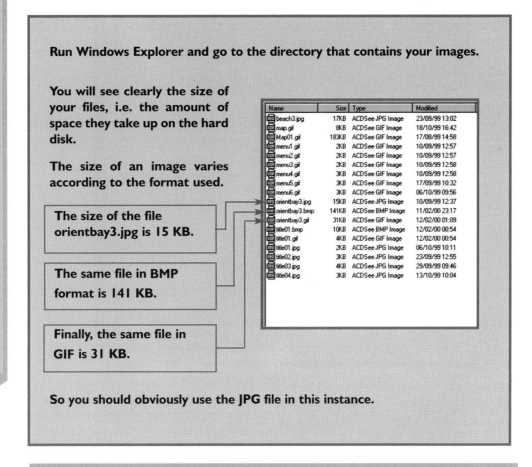

Name	Size	Type	Modified
beach3.jpg	17KB	ACDSee JPG Image	23/09/99 13:02
map.gif	8KB	ACDSee GIF Image	18/10/99 16:42
Map01.gif	183KB	ACDSee GIF Image	17/08/99 14:58
menu1.gif	2KB	ACDSee GIF Image	10/09/99 12:57
menu2.gif	2KB	ACDSee GIF Image	10/09/99 12:57
menu3.gif	2KB	ACDSee GIF Image	10/09/99 12:58
menu4.gif	3KB	ACDSee GIF Image	10/09/99 12:58
menu5.gif	3KB	ACDSee GIF Image	17/09/99 10:32
menu6.gif	3KB	ACDSee GIF Image	06/10/99 09:56
orientbay3.jpg	15KB	ACDSee JPG Image	10/09/99 12:37
orientbay3.bmp	141KB	ACDSee BMP Image	11/02/00 23:17
orientbay3.gif	31KB	ACDSee GIF Image	12/02/00 01:09
title01.bmp	10KB	ACDSee BMP Image	12/02/00 00:54
title01.gif	4KB	ACDSee GIF Image	12/02/00 00:54
title01.jpg	2KB	ACDSee JPG Image	06/10/99 10:11
title02.jpg	3KB	ACDSee JPG Image	23/09/99 12:55
title03.jpg	4KB	ACDSee JPG Image	29/09/99 09:46
title04.jpg	3KB	ACDSee JPG Image	13/10/99 10:04

The size of the file orientbay3.jpg is 15 KB.

The same file in BMP format is 141 KB.

Finally, the same file in GIF is 31 KB.

So you should obviously use the JPG file in this instance.

The time necessary to load an image depends on the type of Internet connection used (modem, cable, ADSL, dedicated connection, etc.) and the quality of the connection between your computer and your Internet Service Provider (bandwidth). For example, the downloading of an image of 50 KB will take about 7 seconds with a 56K modem.

Loading time

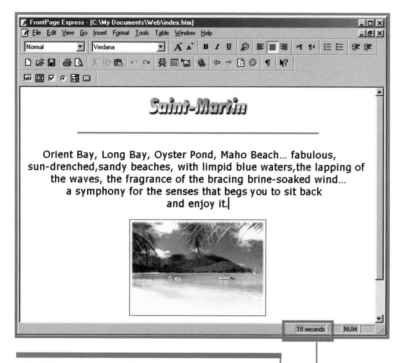

The Web site homepage will take about 18 seconds to load.

Microsoft FrontPage indicates the time it would take to load the page under construction. This information is approximate but gives you a rough idea of the volume of data your site contains. It is shown in the lower right hand corner.

You should practice reducing the size of an image by converting it into *JPG* and tinkering with the compression rate.

Images digitised with a scanner can become unusually big if we do not take some precautions. At the time of scanning the image, select a resolution of 72 dpi (dots per inch). It is not necessary to use a higher resolution for images that are meant to be displayed on the Internet. The 72 figure corresponds to the resolution of most computer screens.

Therefore, scanning a photo at 200 dpi is not necessary, unless you want to work on the image. In that case, it is advisable to use the highest possible resolution so as to conserve fine details in the image. Modify the image using an image-processing software package. Once the image is finalised, reduce it to the desired size and save it in JPG format.

Tip

Low resolution images

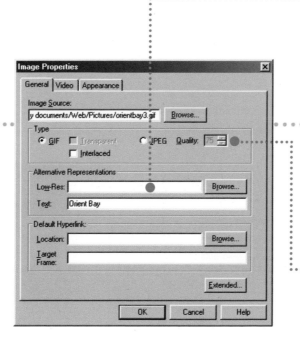

But should you use a second, low-resolution image to get your visitor to wait? Using this method means adding the time it takes to load the low-resolution image to the initial loading time. In spite of your good intentions, your image will now take even longer to load!

If one of your images takes a long time to load, your immediate response might be to trim it down (reduce the size of the image or the number of colours, increase the compression rate, etc.). But if the image remains persistently large in spite of all this, you should then ask yourself whether it should be used on your Web site at all.

Checklist

When you insert an image in a Web page, you can specify a second image at a lower resolution (*Edit/Image Properties*).

This second image must be highly compressed in order to give a fast loading time. This will give your visitors the impression that they can load your Web site quickly, as they will see an image appear quite rapidly.

You can create a low-resolution image by simply converting it into *JPG* and then lowering the quality considerably.

Transparent GIFs

In addition to providing a high compression rate, the *GIF* format can also make the background of images transparent. Why should you want to do this? Just follow the example.

Let us take the Saint-Martin site, and suppose that we want to insert the emblem of the island in place of the image.

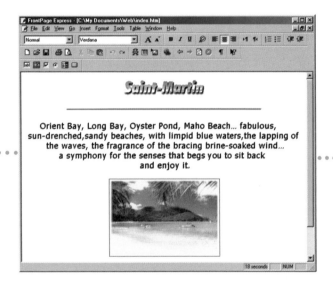

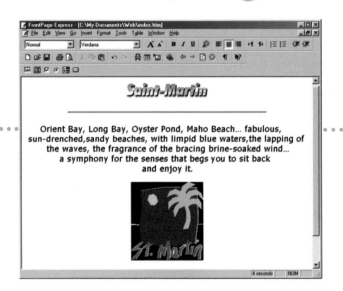

This result is rather disappointing. The black background clashes with the purple of the logo.

Transparent GIFs (continued)

The idea is to create a transparent background with Microsoft Paint.

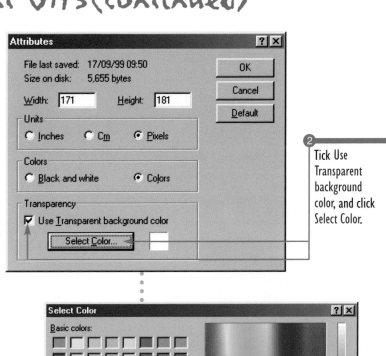

❶ Click the Image menu, then Attributes.

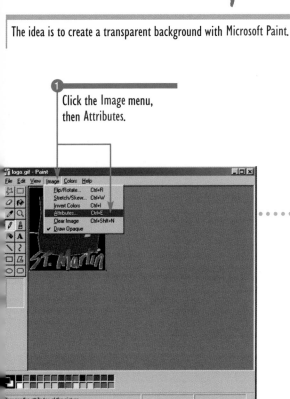

❷ Tick Use Transparent background color, and click Select Color.

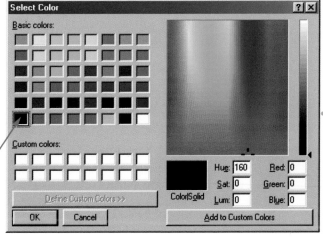

❸ We want to make the black colour transparent. Click on the black-coloured square, and click on OK. Save the image and replace the old one with the new in your Web page.

Transparent GIFs (Conclusion)

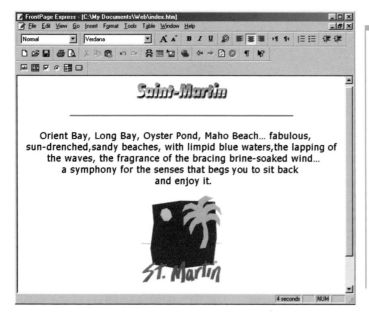

The site looks much better like this.

The background will be transparent when the image is viewed with a browser. The background will usually retain its original colour when you view it in the drawing application.

In some cases, the transparency effect cannot be seen even in Microsoft FrontPage Express. So you should use a browser to test it before you conclude that the transparency effect did not work.

You can cancel the transparent effect by double clicking on the image. Once you have saved the page, the image will be saved without a transparent background. To return to the transparent mode, you will have to use a drawing application such as *Microsoft Paint*.

This transparent mode can only be applied to the GIF format. So if you are using images in other formats (JPG, BMP, etc.), you will have to convert them.

With Paint Shop Pro 5.0 and later versions, you determine the transparent colour with the command Color/ Set Palette Transparency. You must then indicate the number of the colour you want to make transparent. You can use the eyedropper tool to find out the number attributed to a colour. With versions earlier than Paint Shop Pro 5.0, the transparency is defined when the image is saved as a GIF. An options button can be used to select the transparent background colour.

Animated GIFs

Animated GIFs are images in *GIF* format, of course, which are animated when viewed with a browser like *Netscape Navigator* or *Internet Explorer*. The same image, viewed with a drawing application such as *Paint Shop Pro*, on the other hand, will not be animated!

Animated GIFs are used very widely on the Internet to breathe some life into static Web sites.

You should nonetheless use *animated GIFs* sparingly, as they tend to be rather large. This is as they are composed of several images that create the illusion of animated sequences.

The Internet abounds with public domain images. So if you are looking for such resources, you have come to the right place.

If you enter "gif" or "animated gif" as your keywords in a search engine, you will get so many results that you will not know what to do.

A public domain photograph is an image you can use on a Web site free of charge.

http://freeclutter.snap.com
http://www.animationlibrary.com
http://www.baysidecomputing.com
http://www.eclipsed.com
http://www.graphsearch.com
http://www.oposa.com/gallery/frames.htm
http://www.ssanimation.com/site

Background images

File / Page Properties / Background

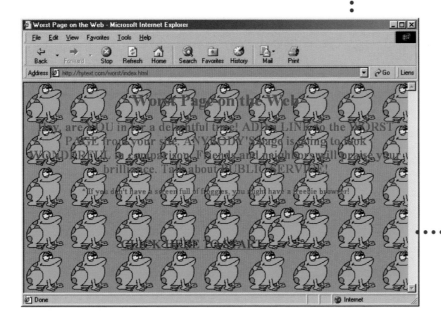

A common technique in Web site design is to use an image for the background. Appealing as the idea may sound, you have to choose the right type of image for this purpose. Many a Web site turns out a disaster because the background image makes it illegible.

This site is a typical example of what should not be done. The text and the images seem to merge. The background image is unnecessarily aggressive and repetitive. The text is, therefore, hard to read.

.....Background images (continued) ......

Let us illustrate this phenomenon in our tourism Web site. One of the pages of the sites lists a few highly recommended hotels for a dream stay on this paradise island. The page was designed without a background image.

① The page is a little dull. Click File/Page Properties, and select Background.

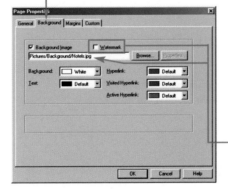

② Select Background Image. If you do tick the Watermark option, the image will be repeated until it covers the full width of the window.

The background image has to be made clearer. Using Paint Shop Pro, you are going to enlarge it until it covers the full width of the window, and thus avoid an unsightly repetition (*Watermark* option in the *Background* tab).

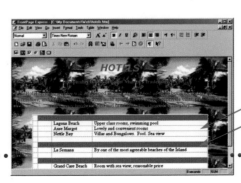

③ The text has become illegible. To remedy this problem, the cells of the table were made white and light green. Nevertheless, the page is far too dark.

Creating a background image

CHAPTER 6 : TIPS AND TECHNIQUES

1 Open the image in Paint Shop Pro and select View/Image

2 The dimensions of the image are clearly indicated. Click OK then click Image/Resize to resize the image.

3 Create an image 800 pixels wide. The height is adjusted automatically if you have ticked the option Maintain aspect ratio.

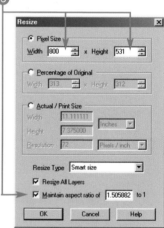

4 The image is now much larger.

5 The image cannot be used as is because the background is too dark. It should be lightened so that the text can be read easily. Click Colors/Adjust/Brightness and Contrast to make the images clearer.

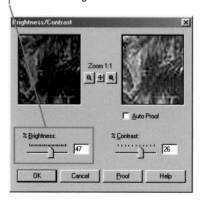

6 Now save the image in JPG format, with File/Save As. Click Options to improve the compression rate.

Changing the compression rate

The initial size of the image was 256 × 170 pixels. The new image is 800 × 531 pixels! The time it will take to load the image has gone up a lot, therefore.

To avoid this, the image was saved at a very high rate of compression. The quality of the image has suffered as a result, but as this is a background image and very bright, the loss of quality is not really visible. In the end, the new image is the same size as the old one, i.e. 20 KB.

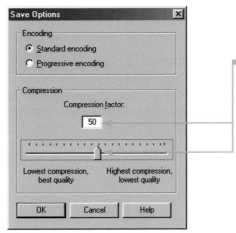

Select a high compression rate. The image will suffer loss of quality, but as it will be used as a background, the lack of detail will not matter.

Insert the new image into the Web page. Your page is now much easier to read than before. As a Webmaster, you must never neglect how the pages of your Web site look.

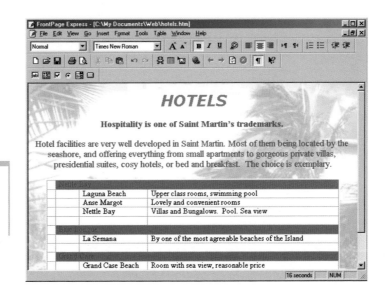

Background music

With FrontPage Express you can also insert background music into your Web pages. This function will only work with Internet Explorer. The background music will not be heard with Netscape Navigator. For this reason, background music should be used sparingly.

There are several audio file formats, just as there are several image formats.... You should however only use .MID, .WAV and .AU formats in your Web pages.

By definition, a WAV file, i.e. a file with the extension .WAV, takes up much space on a hard disk, and will take a long time to load. So you should avoid inserting very large files.

MIDI files (with extension .MID) on the other hand are more suitable for this purpose, as they are generally small in size.

Here is a list of the main formats

File extension	Format
.AIFF or .AIF	Audio format for Macintosh.
.AU	Audio format for SUN / NEXT.
.IFF	Standard format for Amiga.
.MID or .MIDI	Musical Instrument Digital Interface.
.MOD or .XM	Audio format for Amiga.
.MP3 or .MP4 or .MP2	MPEG Layer 3 - 2 - 1.
.RPM or .RA or .RM	Real Audio format.
.WAV or .WAVE	Audio format for Windows.

Introduction to MIDI

MIDI stands for Musical Instrument Digital Interface. It is a convention for communicating musical compositions. The MIDI language does not use the conventional representation of music with its notes and staves. Instead, it encodes sound, and provides information about the pitch of the sound, its length and the instrument used to play it. For instance, it will describe how, in a certain piece, a "C" note must be played loud, in the second octave, for four seconds, by instrument number 079 (i.e. the ocarina). The music is created using the computer's in-built sounds, so if you change the instrument number, you can hear this same four-second "C" played by an alto saxophone, or a grand piano. Since 1991, each instrument has been attributed a number, which is the same for all computers, and all programs.

Creating background music

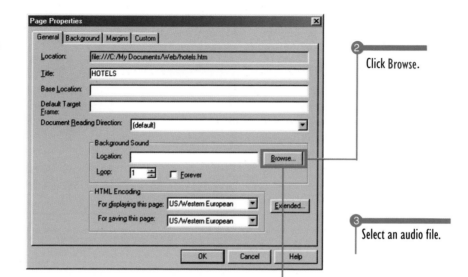

① In FrontPage Express, open the page into which you wish to insert background music, and select File/Page Properties.

② Click Browse.

③ Select an audio file.

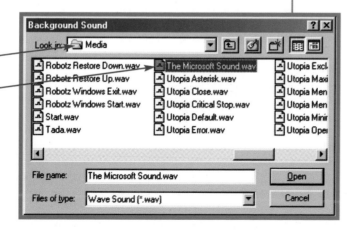

This example shows you precisely what you should not do! The file is not in the working directory of the Web site for one thing, and the name of the file is longer than eight characters. You are strongly advised to use files with no more than 8 characters (plus 3 for the extension).

SOLUTION: Copy The Microsoft Sound.wav into the working directory of your Web site (here C:\My Documents\Web\Sound). The directory \sound will contain all sound extracts used in the Web site. This will help you find your way round more easily afterwards. Now give the file a name with no more than 8 characters, e.g. mssound.wav.

Creating background music (continued)

④ Reinsert the newly re-named, copied file into the directory \sound.

⑤ The access path appears in the Location field.

⑥ Specify how many times you want the music played. Tick Forever if you want it played indefinitely.

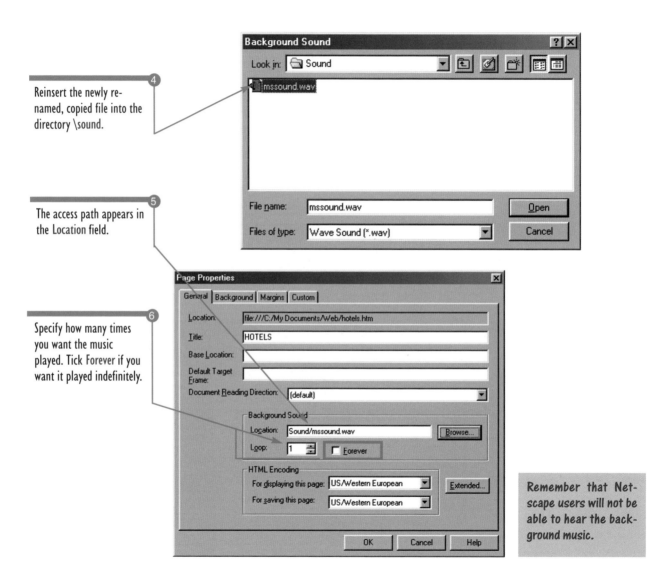

Remember that Net-scape users will not be able to hear the back-ground music.

Chapter 7

Tables

Tables

The construction of the site is progressing rather well. Although our site is limited to just a few pages for the time being, it is relatively easy to offer visitors a proper design, worthy of being published and registered with the leading search engines on the Net. Nevertheless, in constructing your own site, you have undoubtedly noticed the kind of precision required when text appears together with images. Your task will be made much simpler if you use tables.

As in the case of **Microsoft Excel**, a table is composed of cells in which you can place text and images. Once you have defined the structure of your table, text or an image will be placed in each cell, and you will have a far easier time formatting your page.

Place the cursor at the point where you wish to insert a table, then click Table/Insert Table.

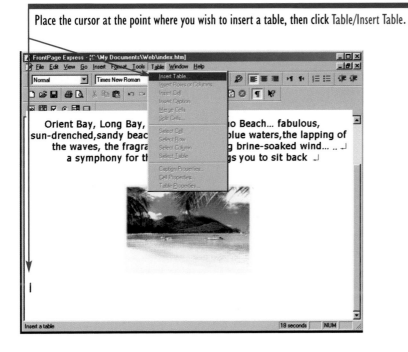

There are no calculation functions as in Excel... A table is not a spread-sheet!

Creating a table

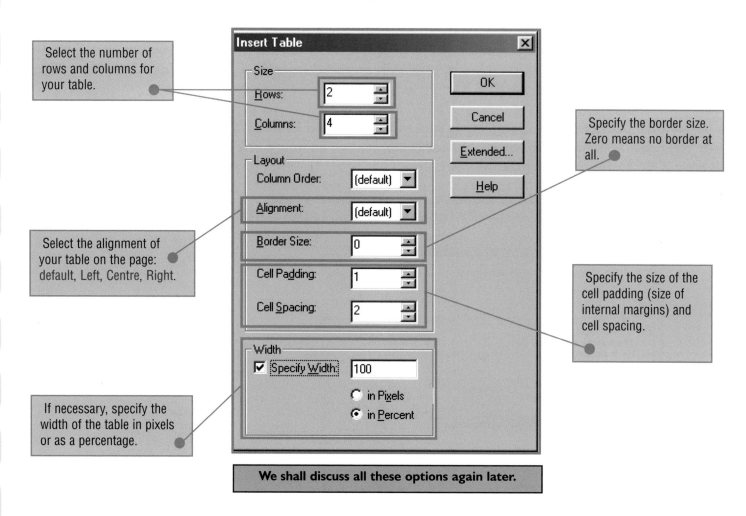

Select the number of rows and columns for your table.

Select the alignment of your table on the page: default, Left, Centre, Right.

If necessary, specify the width of the table in pixels or as a percentage.

Specify the border size. Zero means no border at all.

Specify the size of the cell padding (size of internal margins) and cell spacing.

Insert Table

Size
Rows: 2
Columns: 4

OK
Cancel
Extended...
Help

Layout
Column Order: (default)
Alignment: (default)
Border Size: 0
Cell Padding: 1
Cell Spacing: 2

Width
☑ Specify Width: 100
○ in Pixels
● in Percent

We shall discuss all these options again later.

Displaying a table

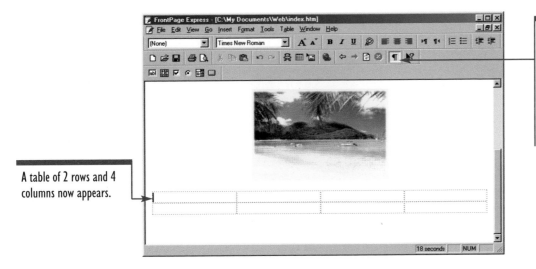

Tick the Show/Hide option to make the table visible in the window. The table will not appear without this option, because we entered a border size of 0 (i.e. no border).

A table of 2 rows and 4 columns now appears.

Another way is to use this icon to create tables with the mouse.

Select the number of rows and columns desired, and the table will take shape in your Web page.

This chapter explains how to work with a table, delete cells and create new ones, split rows or columns, etc.

Basic operations

Inserting a row or a column

Step 1 **Place the cursor in the table and click Table/Insert Rows or Columns.**

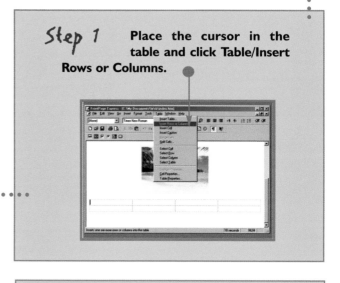

Step 2 **Specify the number of rows or columns you wish to insert.**

Step 3

A new row appears.

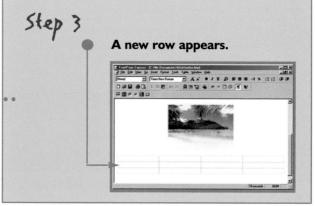

Basic operations (continued)

Selecting a row

Step 1
To select a row:

Place the cursor on one of the cells of the row you wish to select, then click *Select Row* in the *Table* menu.

Step 2
The entire row is selected.

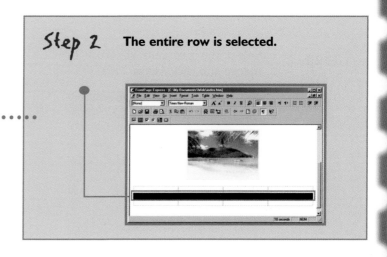

Selecting a column

Step 1
Place the cursor on one of the cells of the column you wish to select, and click *Select Column* in the *Table* menu.

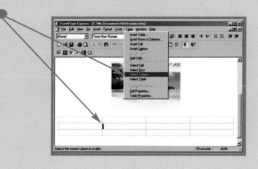

Step 2
The column is selected.

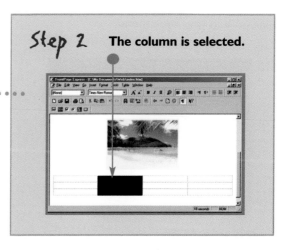

Basic operations (concluded)

Merging cells

Step 1   Select the two cells you wish to merge and click *Merge cells.*

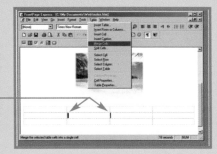

Step 2   The cells are merged.

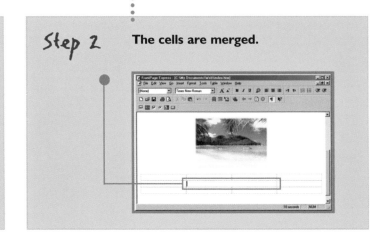

Splitting cells

Step 1   Place the cursor in the cell you wish to split, and click *Split Cells* in the *Table* menu.

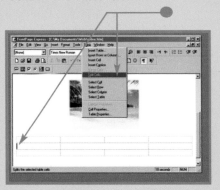

Step 2   Specify the number of cells you wish to add.

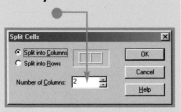

Step 3   The initial cell is split into two.

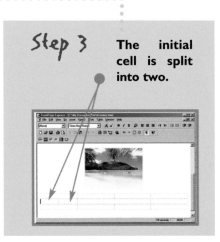

Table Properties

Table / Table Properties

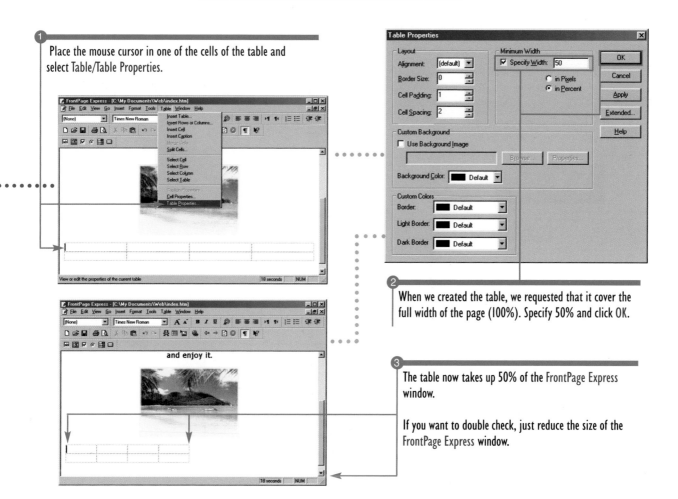

1 Place the mouse cursor in one of the cells of the table and select Table/Table Properties.

2 When we created the table, we requested that it cover the full width of the page (100%). Specify 50% and click OK.

3 The table now takes up 50% of the FrontPage Express window.

If you want to double check, just reduce the size of the FrontPage Express window.

Table Properties (continued)

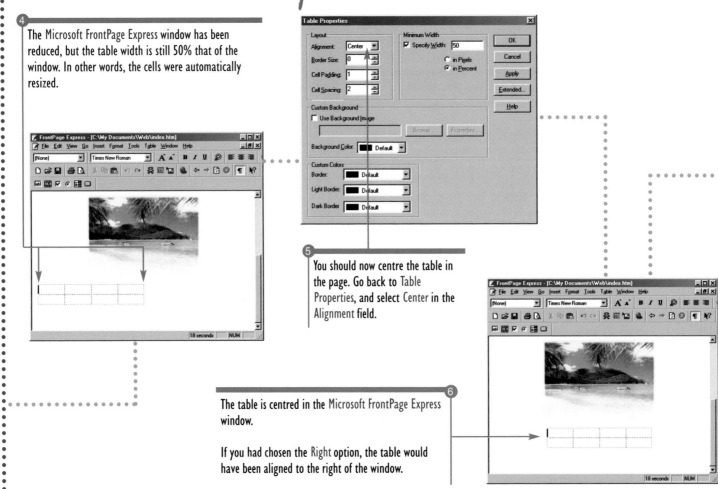

4 The Microsoft FrontPage Express window has been reduced, but the table width is still 50% that of the window. In other words, the cells were automatically resized.

5 You should now centre the table in the page. Go back to Table Properties, and select Center in the Alignment field.

6 The table is centred in the Microsoft FrontPage Express window.

If you had chosen the Right option, the table would have been aligned to the right of the window.

7

Go back to Table Properties again. Do not specify the width.
Untick the corresponding option.

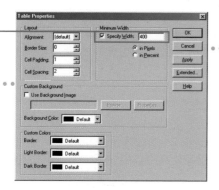

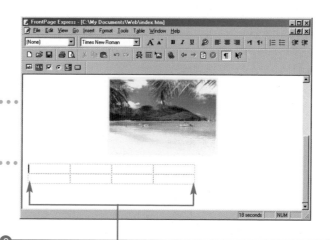

8

The table width is now 400 pixels. The width of the table is no longer given
as a percentage, but is in pixels now, so the cells will not be resized if the
window is reduced.

9

You will note that only the first three cells are visible; the fourth is hidden
because the FrontPage Express window is too narrow.

When you create a table, make sure you do not make it too large, because you
might have to use scroll bars afterwards to view it in its entirety.

10 Go back to the table properties, and do not specify the width of the table.
Untick the corresponding option.

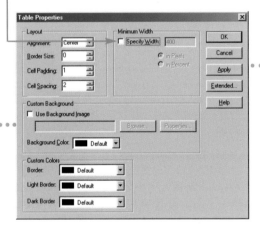

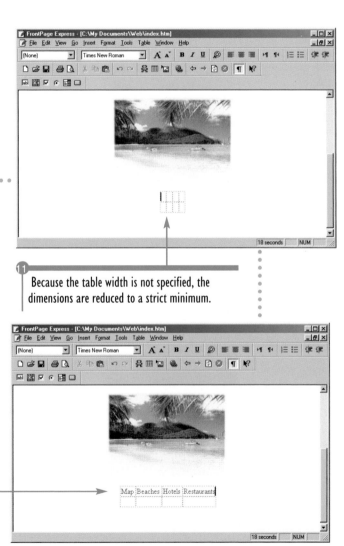

11 Because the table width is not specified, the dimensions are reduced to a strict minimum.

12 The cell width will therefore be proportional to the width of the text entered in the cells.

You can tick the option "Use Background Image" to display an image in the background of your table. This function is not compatible with Microsoft Internet Explorer, however, so you should refrain from using it...

Cell Properties

Table / Cell Properties

In Cell Properties you can define the characteristics of a cell, i.e. the size, the border, the background image, the colour, the alignment of the contents of the cells, etc.

1 To make the site even more attractive, we will replace the text by a more colourful image.

2 Insert an image into each cell of the table (cf. Chapter 5).

Tip

FrontPage Express at times has difficulties displaying the tables, and you might think that they are not constructed properly. To double check, you should view the page in a browser too, and not only in the HTML editor.

You should also select columns or rows with the Table menu options rather than with the mouse, for a more successful result.

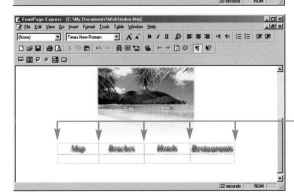

3 The size of the cells depends on the width of the images inserted.

As we have not specified the size of the table, the cell width will be proportional to the width of the images. The images are far too close together, and do not look very good. We can get round the problem by changing the size of each cell. So we will set the cell width to be 10 pixels more than the image width.

It is therefore important to know the size of images inserted into the table.

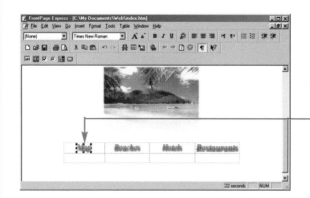

1 Click the first image to select it.

Click Edit/Image Properties.

3 The size of the image is clearly indicated under the Appearance tab.

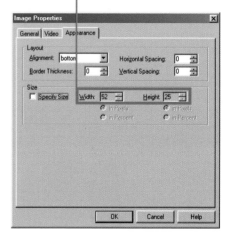

Cell Properties (concluded)

Once you know the size of the image, you can easily change the cell width.

1 Select the first image and click Table/Cell Properties.

2 Specify a cell width of 62 pixels (52+10) and centre the image in the cell.
Remember to tick the option Specify Width.

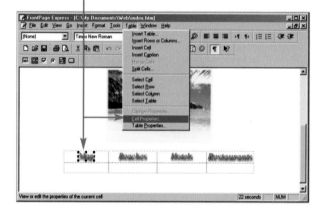

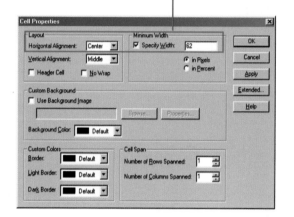

Proceed in the same way for the three other cells.

The cells are spaced out, and your site is made clearer.

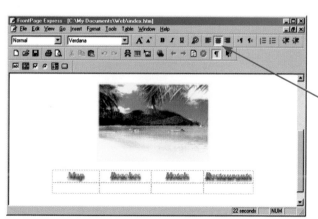

To centre text or an image in a cell, change the properties of the cell and specify a Centre alignment.

Do not use the icon to centre the text. You would be disappointed with the result.

Table of tables

Tables make it a lot easier to construct Web pages. And that isn't all. You can even create a table inside the cell of another table.

Many sites feature a menu, often placed to the left of the page, that can be used to access all the pages of the site rapidly. The Altavista site is a case in point.

The column on the left is used to access the various pages and is displayed on the screen at all times. Information, on the other hand, is shown in the right part of the screen.

This site is well organised and therefore very easy to browse.

One way to construct a site like this is to use tables. We will go over another method presently, which is a little easier to apply...

Let us leave our tourism Web site for now, and focus on creating a site that can be viewed by users with 800 X 600 screen resolution. The choice is debatable, but worth discussing.

The following example shows how the use of tables can simplify laying out Web pages. The text and images are placed in the different cells that have been created. All that is necessary is to visualise the structure of the page in advance and the layout of the different items in it.

(See page 106).

Creating a table

Step 1   The first step consists of creating a table of a single row and two columns. Specify a table width of 800 pixels (Table Properties). Click the first cell and enter a width of 130 pixels (cell properties).

Click the second cell and give a width of 670 pixels (Cell Properties).

(130+670=800).

Specify a left horizontal alignment and a top vertical alignment (Cell Properties).

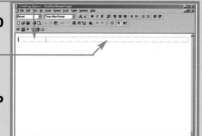

Step 2   Create a table of a single column and two rows in the first cell.

Place the cursor in the first cell (as indicated below) and create a second table of a single column and two rows.

Select the two cells and specify a width of 130 pixels (Cell Properties).

For each cell, specify a left horizontal alignment and a top vertical alignment (Cell Properties).

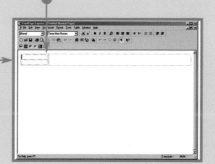

Step 3 Place the cursor in the right-hand cell and create a table of a single column and two rows.

Specify a cell width of 570 pixels.

(570+130=800) (Cell Properties).

Specify a left horizontal alignment and a top vertical alignment (Cell Properties) for each cell.

Step 4 Place the cursor in the top right-hand cell and create a table of 5 columns and a single row.

The 5 cells will each contain an image that will be used as the general menu.

Place the cursor in the second row of the leftmost column.

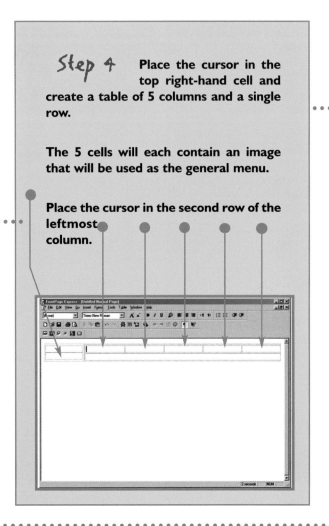

Creating a table (concluded)

Step 5   Create a table of 5 rows (or more) and two columns.

Select the first column and specify a cell width of 13 pixels (Cell Properties).

Select the second column and specify
a cell width of 117 pixels (Cell Properties).

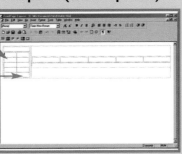

Step 6   The underlying structure
of your page is completed.

All that is left to do now is to place images
and text in each of the cells.

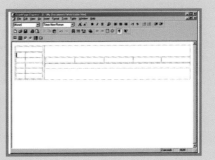

The purpose of this
demonstration is to
show how tables can
be used to create a
Web page. You should
save the structure so
that you do not have to
recreate it every time
for similar pages on the
Web.

Formatting

Rapid access to the pages of the site.

Emblem of Saint Martin.

E-mail address for contacts.

If we take the images of the Saint-Martin Web site and rapidly create a few additional icons, we can easily change the entire presentation of the site with a few clicks of the mouse.

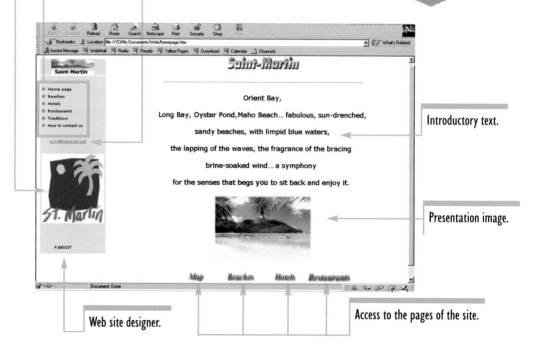

Introductory text.

Presentation image.

With this method, you must design each page in the same way. Only the information in the centre of the screen will be different. Let us assume that in case of the logo, you decide to insert another image. You will then have to make the appropriate changes in all the pages of the site... This makes the site difficult to maintain, requiring a real effort from the Webmaster.

Web site designer.

Access to the pages of the site.

Chapter 8

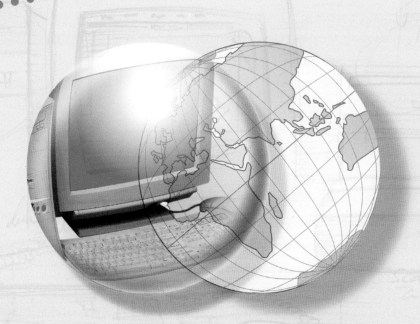

Hypertext links

Introduction

AWeb site is built out of hyperlinks. **A link is a word or image on which you click in order to access a new Web page.**

The Yahoo search directory features an impressive number of links on a single page.

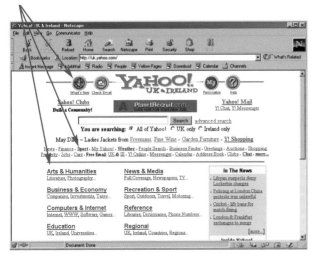

Remember that the Internet is based on hypertext technology which makes it possible to access various documents by clicking with the mouse. An underlined word or an image framed with a blue border, which may or may not be visible, indicates a link. You can identify a hypertext link by the cursor's change of appearance.

Links enable Net surfers to skip from page to page. The tourism site for Saint-Martin would require at least 4 hyperlinks. But you, as a Webmaster, can always add more, for example to provide access to other Web sites or resources directly related (one hopes!) to the site.

You should determine in advance the number of pages you want on your site and create them using Microsoft FrontPage Express. Once you have designed the documents, it is easy to relate them to each other with hypertext links.

As the purpose of this book is not to show how to create the site given in the example, but rather how to create any Web site, we will not delve further into the other pages. They were built in the same way as was the welcome page, using tables, images, text, etc.

Structure of a site

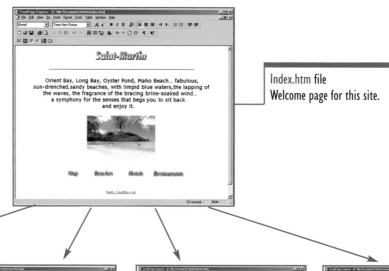

Index.htm file
Welcome page for this site.

Map.htm **file :**
Access to a map and a geopolitical description of the island.

Beaches.htm **file :**
Access to a page about the beaches.
In this example, a link will be created from the word "beaches" in the introductory text.

Hotels.htm **file :**
Access to a page listing the main hotels.

Restaurant.page **file**
Access to a page listing restaurants and other attractions on the island.

It is now time to insert the links into the Web page on our site. There are two cases to consider when doing this with *Microsoft FrontPage Express*: either the two pages already exist, or else you have to create the second page when you insert the link. Let's look at the first alternative.

Inserting a hyperlink

Insert / Hyperlink

```
  Cascade
  Tile
  Arrange Icons
✔ 1 C:\My Documents\Web\index.htm
  2 C:\My Documents\Web\beaches.htm
```

1 Start by opening the page on the island's beaches (File/Open).

Use the Window menu to make sure that the two pages have been opened in Microsoft FrontPage Express.

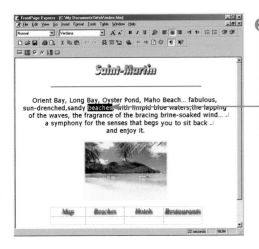

2 Select the word you want to use as the hyperlink. Double clicking on a word will select it automatically.

3 Select Insert, then Hyperlink.

A hyperlink often consists of one word, but you can choose to use several words or a whole sentence.

Checklist

1. The *Open Pages* tab lets you choose a target page already opened in *Microsoft FrontPage Express*. You must therefore open it first with *File/Open*.

2. The *World Wide Web* tab lets you specify a target page from an external Web site.

3. For example: http://www.yahoo.com

   The *New Page* tab lets you specify a target page which does not yet exist. The page will therefore be automatically created.

Properties of a link

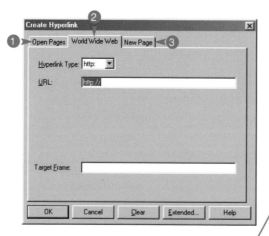

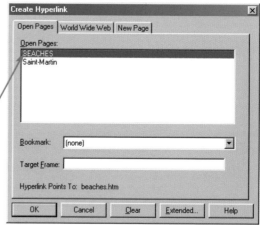

Click on the Open Pages tab and choose the target page from the list.

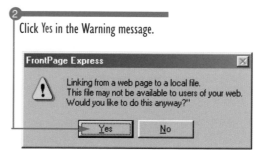

Click Yes in the Warning message.

The link has been created. When you click on "beaches" in the introductory text, the browser will display the second page of the site.

A hyperlink can also consist of an image.

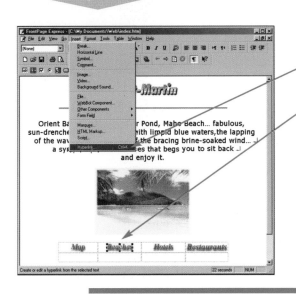

1 Use the mouse to select the image you want to use as a hyperlink, then click **Insert / Hyperlink**.

2 Click on the **Open Pages** tab and select the page.

3 Click **Yes** in the warning message.

Summary

The underlining shows clearly that the word "beaches" has become a hyperlink.

Two links have been created: one using a word ("beaches") on the welcome page, and the other using an image on the site (beaches). These two links provide access to the same Web page, the one about the beaches of Saint-Martin.

1 Hold down the Ctrl key and click on the link to test it. Do the same thing with the image of the beaches.

Notice that the image is not underlined. It's hard to tell that it is a hyperlink, though the cursor changes from a pointer to a hand.

2 Double click on the image to change its properties, and specify a border 2 pixels wide in the Appearance tab.

This time, the image is framed with a blue border, which indicates the presence of a hyperlink. Whether you use a blue border is purely your aesthetic decision.

Different kinds of links

Links enable your visitors to go through the various pages of the site. But why not take advantage of the opportunity to provide your visitors access to other Web sites or Internet resources or, for example, allow them to contact the site's Webmaster by e-mail?

1 Create a third row in the table at the bottom of the page and merge the four cells.

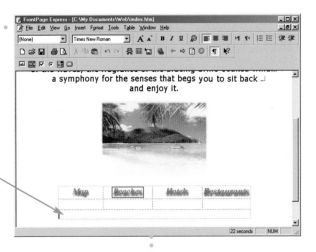

2 Enter the e-mail address so that Net surfers can contact the site's Webmaster. Centre the text in the cell (Table/Cell Properties/Centre).

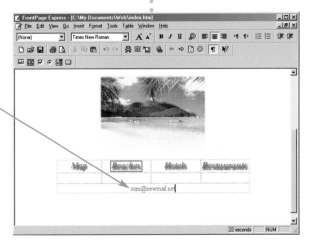

Different kinds of links (continued)

③ Underline the e-mail address and create a hyperlink (Insert/Hyperlink).

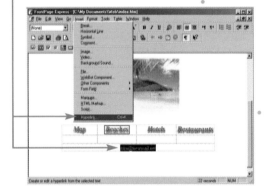

④ In the Hyperlink Type dialogue box, choose the Mailto: item and enter the e-mail address.

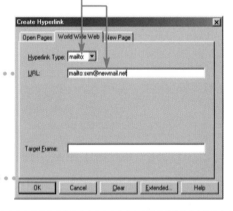

⑤ The blue underlining indicates that the link has been created.

Save the page and test this link: press the Ctrl key, and click on the e-mail address. A message says that Microsoft FrontPage Express only allows testing of HTTP links.

You should now test the page under real conditions of use with your favourite browser.

Different kinds of links (concluded)

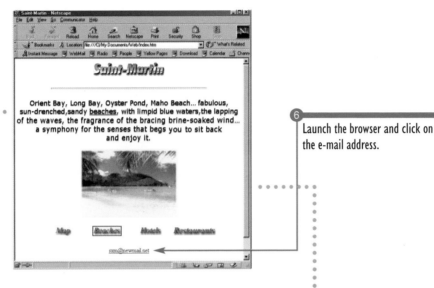

6 Launch the browser and click on the e-mail address.

7 The messaging program starts automatically so that a visitor to your site can e-mail you easily.

Downloading files

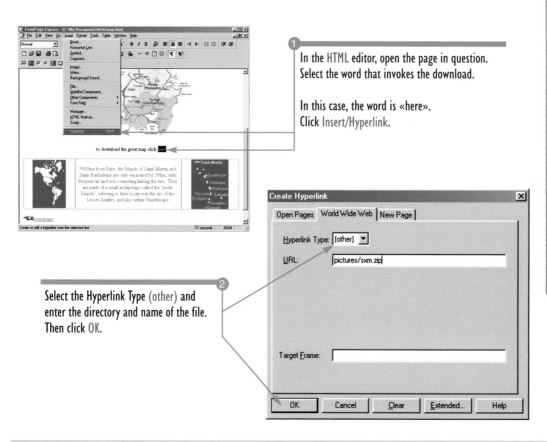

1 In the HTML editor, open the page in question. Select the word that invokes the download.

In this case, the word is «here».
Click Insert/Hyperlink.

2 Select the Hyperlink Type (other) and enter the directory and name of the file. Then click OK.

A Web site is not just a window. Suppose we want the visitor to be able to download a map of Saint-Martin.
This can be done from the map.htm page by clicking on the word "here" (see example).

This map is an image in *JPG* format compressed using WinZip. That's why the file is called sxm.zip. Only someone wanting to use the map will have to wait as it downloads.

The material you want to make available for download is in the file «C:\My Documents\Web\Images\sxm.zip. Now, as the site's map.htm file is in C:\My Documents\Web, all you have to do is enter "images/sxm.zip".

Testing the download

1

Launch your favourite browser and test the link you just created.

Click on the word "here" to download the file.

2

The browser opens a window from which you can save the file on your hard disk. The test has been successful; the simulated downloading has occurred.

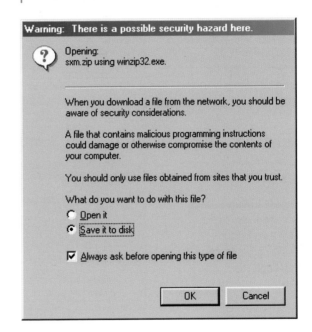

Tip

We can download any type of file: images, musical excerpts, photographs, Microsoft Word documents, etc.

Links from an image

Changing a link from an image is done in the same way: double-click on the image to see its properties or click on Edit/Image Properties.

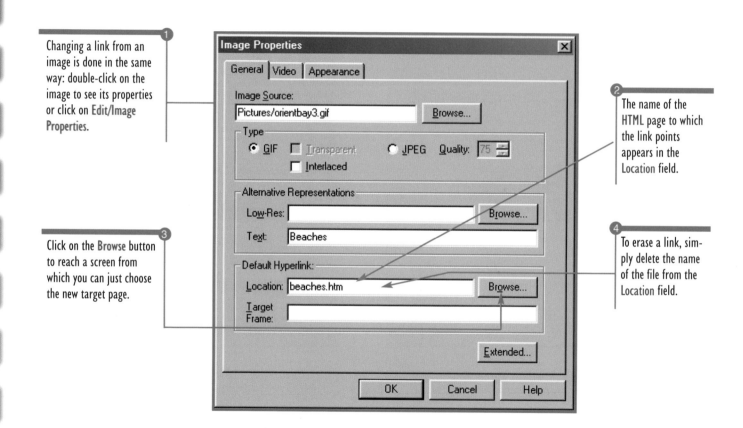

The name of the HTML page to which the link points appears in the Location field.

Click on the Browse button to reach a screen from which you can just choose the new target page.

To erase a link, simply delete the name of the file from the Location field.

Image Properties

General | Video | Appearance

Image Source:
Pictures/orientbay3.gif   Browse...

Type
● GIF   □ Transparent   ○ JPEG   Quality: 75
        □ Interlaced

Alternative Representations
Low-Res: Browse...
Text: Beaches

Default Hyperlink:
Location: beaches.htm   Browse...
Target
Frame:

Extended...

OK   Cancel   Help

Edit / clear a hyperlink

You can edit a link at any time and move it to another page of the site, or delete it altogether. To do any of these things, you have to use *Edit/Link Properties*.

1

Make sure that Microsoft FrontPage Express has already loaded the target page for the link you want to edit.

If you want to move this link to point to another page, make sure that that page is in memory.

Using the mouse, place the cursor on the link you want to edit and click Edit/Link Properties.

In this case, you are going to remove the link from the word "beaches" on the welcome page.

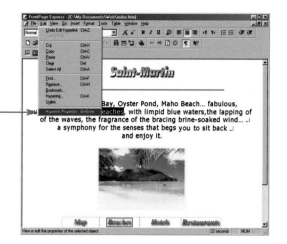

2

Select the new target page, then click OK.

To delete the link, click the Clear button, then OK.

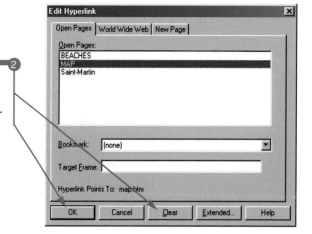

Inserting a link to a bookmark

Let's take a look at the "Virtual Saint-Martin" Web site to illustrate this principle. The restaurant.htm page contains a selective list of restaurants located on Saint-Martin. The list is long and therefore hard to browse. The idea is to create bookmarks that take you directly to the restaurants located in a certain town or region on the island. The first step is to decide where to put these bookmarks.

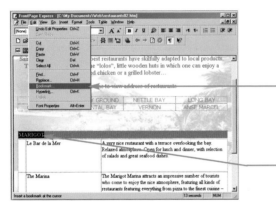

1 Select a word in the page that marks the beginning of some part of the text.

In this case, there is a bookmark placed at the beginning of each table heading.

A Web page containing a lot of text and images can turn out to be hard to read. You will actually have to scroll the document with the vertical scroll bars. One way of getting round this problem is to use bookmarks. A bookmark is an invisible mark that lets you define a particular spot on a Web page. You can then easily create a link that points directly to that particular part of the Web page, and therefore access that portion of the page immediately.

2 The default bookmark name is the word thus selected. However, you can change this name.
Next, click OK.

3 The word is then underscored with a dotted line, which indicates the presence of a bookmark in that location.

Inserting a link to a bookmark

Proceed in the same way for the other bookmarks on the page. Once you have placed the bookmarks where you want them, it is easy to create a link that points to a particular bookmark.

All the bookmarks have been set. You can delete one by choosing it from the list and clicking on Clear.

Bookmark

Bookmark Name:

`oriental`

Clear

Other Bookmarks on this Page:

MARIGOT
oriental
sandy
nettle
long
case
marcel
vernon

Goto

OK

Cancel

Help

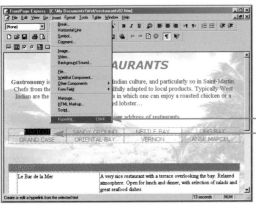

4

You should now make the links. To do this, create a table listing the different towns where the best restaurants are found.

Select the first word, here "MARIGOT" and create a link (Insert/Hyperlink).

5

The target page is the same one from which the link has been created.

In the drop-down menu, select the bookmark "MARIGOT".

Create Hyperlink

Open Pages | World Wide Web | New Page

Open Pages:
RESTAURANTS

Bookmark: MARIGOT

Target Frame:

Hyperlink Points To: #MARIGOT

OK   Cancel   Clear   Extended...   Help

Repeat this operation for all the other bookmarks. Create links that point to the corresponding bookmarks. In this example, the bookmarks are placed on the same page as the links, but you can also have a link pointing to a bookmark on another page.

Testing a bookmark

1 The eight links have been created and point to the bookmarks on the Web page.

While holding down the Ctrl key, test one of the links, for example "SANDY GROUND".

2 The file is displayed automatically so that the beginning of the marked section appears at the top. In this way, Net users go directly to the part that interests them, without having to scroll through the whole document.

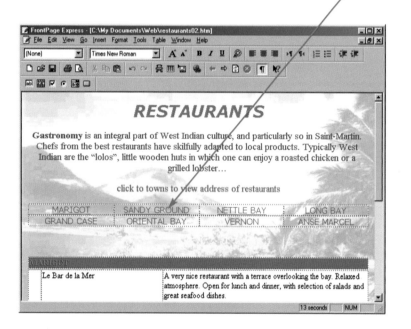

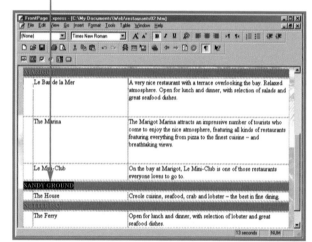

Chapter 9

Image maps

Introduction

An image map is an image from which various Web pages can be accessed by using the mouse to place the cursor at different points within the image. Normally, when you create a link from an image you, as the Webmaster, choose one and only one target page. With an image map, the target page accessed depends on the place where you click with the mouse.

The restaurant.htm page shows how this works.

When you click on one of the towns in the table, you access directly the corresponding list of restaurants.

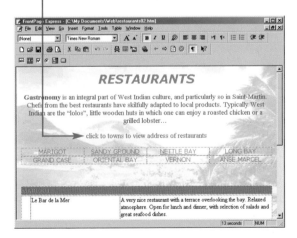

It would be much nicer for the Web user to see a map of the island from which to choose a town.

Delete the table and replace it with a map (with a transparent background, in this case). The name of the file is mapxm.gif.

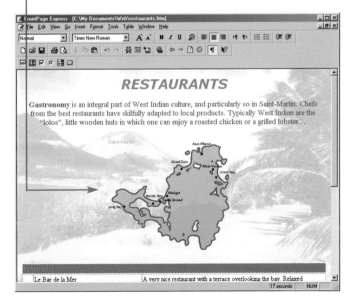

Creating an image map

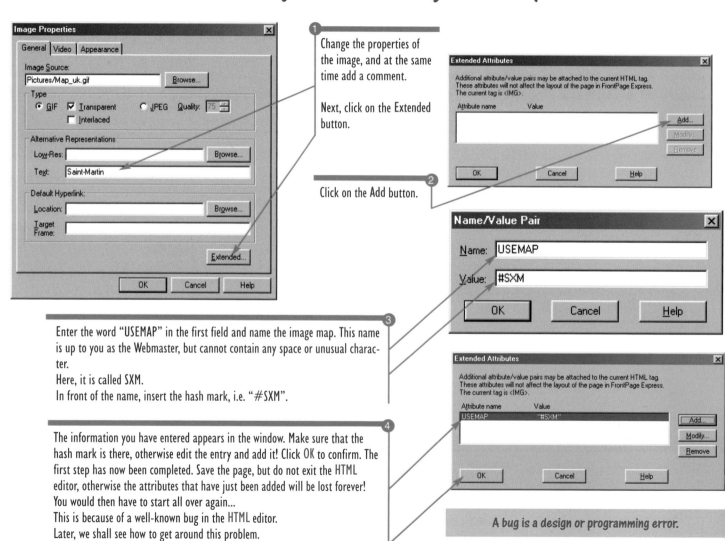

1 Change the properties of the image, and at the same time add a comment.

Next, click on the Extended button.

2 Click on the Add button.

3 Enter the word "USEMAP" in the first field and name the image map. This name is up to you as the Webmaster, but cannot contain any space or unusual character.
Here, it is called SXM.
In front of the name, insert the hash mark, i.e. "#SXM".

4 The information you have entered appears in the window. Make sure that the hash mark is there, otherwise edit the entry and add it! Click OK to confirm. The first step has now been completed. Save the page, but do not exit the HTML editor, otherwise the attributes that have just been added will be lost forever! You would then have to start all over again...
This is because of a well-known bug in the HTML editor.
Later, we shall see how to get around this problem.

A bug is a design or programming error.

Image maps

We must now define the areas of the image corresponding to the *HTML* pages to be displayed.

These areas are defined in terms of pixels. We can distinguish three types of area: circles, rectangles and polygons. In our site, we will use only circles.

1 In the example opposite, circles have been drawn but they do not appear. They are there only to make the principle of using image maps easier to understand.

Whenever a Net user clicks within one of the eight circles, one of the eight corresponding HTML files is launched. If the user clicks outside the circles, nothing happens.

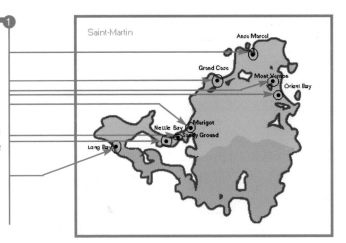

2 We use Microsoft Paint to determine the co-ordinates of the circles that define the various hot spots.

In this case, the cursor is pointing to the town of Marigot.

The co-ordinates appear in terms of pixels at the bottom of the Microsoft Paint screen.

Take note of them, because they will be used to define the first hot spot. Proceed in the same way for the other areas on the map. Place the cursor on each of the points and note down the co-ordinates. Once all the points on the map have been determined, you can then enter the appropriate HTML code for the Web page.

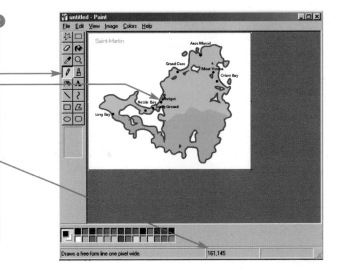

Editing the HTML code

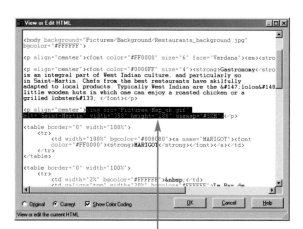

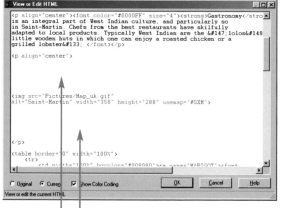

1 Go back to Microsoft FrontPage Express and display the HTML code (View/HTML).

2 Locate the HTML text referring to the image. In this case, it is mapsxm.gif.

3 Insert several blank lines before and after in order to isolate this part clearly. This will make it easier to distinguish the various HTML elements.

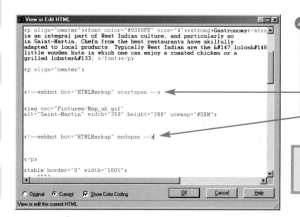

4 Insert the following line in front of the text block:
   <!--webbot bot="HTMLMarkup" startspan -->

And this line after the text block:
   <!--webbot bot="HTMLMarkup" endspan -->

<!--webbot bot="HTMLMarkup" startspan -->
<!--webbot bot="HTMLMarkup" endspan -->

We insert the two *HTML* commands shown here in order to prevent *Microsoft FrontPage Express* from interpreting the content between them. In this way you as the Webmaster can write whatever you wish, without having the *HTML* editor try to check the syntax. This will get around the well-known bug already mentioned.

Editing the HTML code

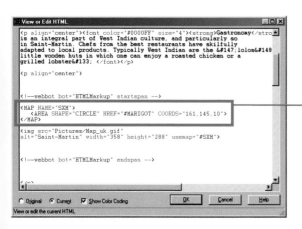

Complete the page using the following HTML commands:

```
<MAP NAME="SXM">
   <AREA SHAPE="CIRCLE" HREF="#MARIGOT" COORDS="161,145,10">
   </MAP>
```

This line indicates the presence of a hot spot. This area is a circle (SHAPE="CIRCLE"), with centre at coordinates (161,145) and with radius 10 pixels. The coordinates were determined using Microsoft Paint.

When you click inside the circle, you will launch the "MARIGOT" link. This invokes not a Web page, but a bookmark (see Inserting a link to a bookmark). Instead of the "Marigot" bookmark, we could have specified a Web page, for example:

```
<AREA SHAPE="CIRCLE" HREF="http://www.yahoo.com/" COORDS="161,145,10"
```

Complete the page using the coordinates of the other reactive areas, click OK and save the page.

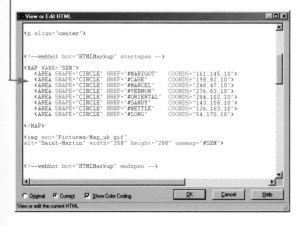

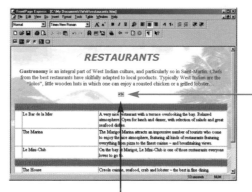

Once you have left the previous screen, and its image has disappeared, an icon appears, generated by the two lines that frame the HTML code that was entered. Since FrontPage Express does not change the syntax, it can only display what is contained therein.

Double click on the icon to view or edit the HTML code behind it.

Testing the image map

Now use your regular browser to make sure that the image map is working.

Click each of the defined areas and make sure that the HTML page is displayed correctly.

In this case, the page must be displayed in such a way that the part of the table relating to the area on which you have clicked appears at the top.

We can see how mages map make it easy to access various pages on the Web site.

For example, a company could put a single composite picture of all its products on line. Visitors could obtain a detailed description of any one of them, by clicking on it. Thus, the company would not have to provide an individual picture of each product.

Summary

To sum up, the *HTML* page contains the commands below. Pay special attention to the case in which the bookmarks are written, i.e. to whether capitals or small letters are used (upper or lower case).

These bookmarks were created using capital letters, and so they had to be entered in capitals in the *HTML* code... Otherwise, a mouse click in one of the areas would not work.

```
<!--webbot bot="HTMLMarkup" startspan -->

<MAP NAME="SXM">
        <AREA SHAPE="CIRCLE" HREF="#MARIGOT" COORDS="161,145,10">
        <AREA SHAPE="CIRCLE" HREF="#CASE" COORDS="198,82,10">
        <AREA SHAPE="CIRCLE" HREF="#MARCEL" COORDS="248,47,10">
        <AREA SHAPE="CIRCLE" HREF="#VERNON" COORDS="276,83,10">
        <AREA SHAPE="CIRCLE" HREF="#ORIENTALE" COORDS="284,102,10">
        <AREA SHAPE="CIRCLE" HREF="#SANDY" COORDS="143,158,10">
        <AREA SHAPE="CIRCLE" HREF="#NETTLE" COORDS="126,163,10">
        <AREA SHAPE="CIRCLE" HREF="#LONGUE" COORDS="54,170,10">
</MAP>

<img src="images/cartesxm.gif"
alt="Ile de Saint-Martin, French section" width="358"
height="288" usemap="#SXM">

<!--webbot bot="HTMLMarkup" endspan -->
```

The **SHAPE** attribute of the **<AREA>** tag has three possible values, each corresponding to different meanings of the **COORDS** attribute:

CIRCLE	The centre of the circle and the radius (in pixels).
RECT	The upper left-hand corner and lower right-hand corner of the rectangle.
POLY	Each vertex of the polygon.

Example: To create a hot spot in the shape of a rectangle:

```
<AREA SHAPE="RECT" COORDS="50,50,150,200" HREF="http://www.yahoo.com/">
```

Image map: Points to remember

Creating an image map is not complicated in itself. However, we have to admit that FrontPage Express does not exactly simplify this task. For one thing, you have to get around one of the bugs in the program which does not retain the HTML commands added "manually". Furthermore, it was not originally designed to handle image maps. FrontPage 2000 does however simplify this matter.

So let us go over once again the procedure for creating an image map. Take care not to leave FrontPage Express until the following six steps have been completed.

1. Insert an image and locate the areas (circle, rectangle, polygon) from which the HTML pages will be launched.

2. Edit the attributes of the image and add the keyword **USEMAP**, then give it a name preceded by the hash mark (#).

3. Note down the exact coordinates of the hot spots using Microsoft Paint. (You could also use Paint Shop Pro.)

4. Edit the HTML code and get around the FrontPage Express bug.

5. Item by item, add the HTML code corresponding to each hot spot. Specify the co-ordinates of each area in pixels.

6. Use a browser to test the image map.

Chapter 10

Frames

Introduction

Up to now, only one Web page at a time has been displayed in the browser. We go from one page to the other by clicking on hypertext links. With frame technology we can divide the browser screen into several areas, each of which is a separate **HTML** file. In this way, several **HTML** pages can be displayed on the same screen.

The advantage of using frames is that you can design a menu, for instance, that remains displayed alongside any page of the Web site. In chapter 7, we saw how to create such menus using tables.

The left-hand column is a menu accessible from any page of the site.

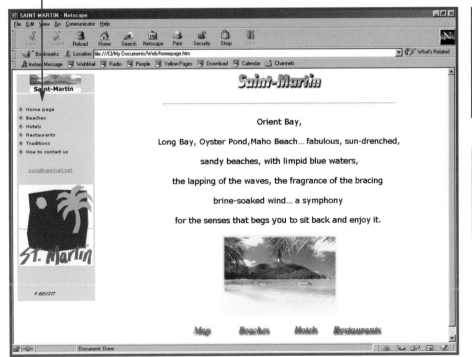

This site consists of only one HTML file. The menu is an integral part of the page. It was designed using tables. Each page of the site has to have the same structure, and comprise the same images and text in the menu.

If you want to make changes to the menu, you will have to revise all the pages of the site, one by one... The more pages the site contains, the harder it is to maintain.

The principle of frames

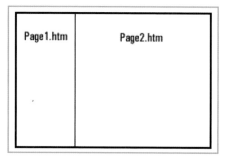

In the browser, two pages will be simulta-neously displayed, but the user is not aware that two different files are involved.

If the contents of the page on the left are changed, only one Web page needs to be updated, not the entire site. This saves a considerable amount of time.

When using frames instead of tables to construct a Web site, you must create at least two Web pages (or obviously more for a multi-page site). One of them represents the menu on the left (*pagel.htm*); the other(s), the pages comprising the site (*page2.htm, page3.htm, page4.htm,* etc.).

Microsoft FrontPage Express cannot be used to manage Web sites built with frames. It cannot display several different pages in the same window - something that most recent browsers can do quite easily. Fortunately, FrontPage 2000 does a splendid job of managing frames.

Must we avoid frames when using Microsoft FrontPage Express? Of course not. We just have to test the site under real conditions of use, i.e. view it with a browser and not merely with the HTML editor.

Be that as it may, a Webmaster will always save the page under construction before viewing it in a browser; otherwise the changes made since the last save will not be taken into account.

Creating a site using frames

Main page: welcome.htm. This file contains only HTML commands. It describes the structure of the site. This is now the new welcome page from which the site is accessed.

Second page: menu02.htm. This page contains the menu that will be displayed on the left.

Paradoxically, to create a site composed of two windows, such as the one presented in the introduction to this chapter, you need not two, but three Web pages! The first file contains the *HTML* commands describing the structure of the windows; the other two files are the Web pages themselves.

The name of the welcome page of the site already built (without frames) is *index.htm*.

From now on, the home page is *welcome.htm*. If we absolutely wanted to keep *index.htm* as the welcome page, we would have had to rename the files involved, and risk making their links obsolete. In general, the problem does not arise, because a Webmaster knows in advance whether or not frames will be used.

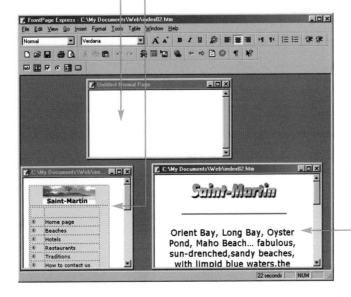

Third page: index02.htm. This page contains the right part of the main page.

Creating frames

Naturally, if you are going to build a site using frames, you have to know a little *HTML*. You don't need to be a programming genius, but you do have to know the basic commands required for building a site.

1 Create a blank page under Microsoft FrontPage Express and save it in the working directory of the site (see Chapter 3).

2 This page now becomes the site's welcome page. Let us call it welcome.htm.

3 Click on View/HTML to view the HTML commands of the newly created page.

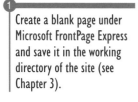

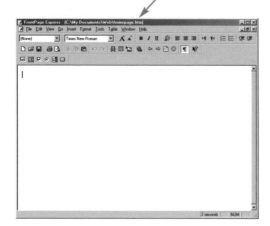

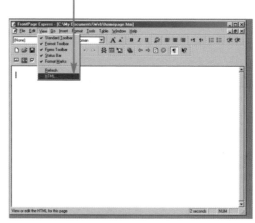

4 Microsoft FrontPage Express displays the HTML commands. Colours are used to distinguish the various elements.

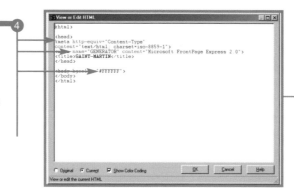

To build a site using frames, all you have to do is to fill in this page with new HTML commands.

This is more of a data-entry than a formatting task.

Editing the HTML code

We will not dwell on **HTML**, which lies beyond the scope of this book. Those wishing to familiarise themselves with **HTML** can study the code as they create their Web pages.

The editor displays the following commands:

```
<html>

<head>
<meta http-equiv="Content-Type"
content="text/html; charset=iso-8859-1">
<meta name="GENERATOR" content="Microsoft FrontPage Express 2.0">
<title> Virtual Saint-Martin - Discovering the Island of Saint-Martin</title>
</head>

<body bgcolor="#FFFFFF">
</body>
</html>
```

Delete the two lines:

```
<body bgcolor="#FFFFFF">
</body>
```

And replace them with the next four lines. It does not matter whether upper or lower case letters are used.

```
<frameset cols="135,*" frameborder="NO" border="0">
 <frame name="left" src="menu02.htm">
 <frame name="right" src="index02.htm">
</frameset>
```

What the code means

<frameset cols = "135,*" frameborder = "NO" border = "0">
This line tells the HTML editor to divide the window in two. The word "COLS" indicates that a page is divided into columns (vertical). The value 135 specifies the width of the left column, i.e. 135 pixels.
The asterisk indicates that the width of the right column corresponds to the remaining width of the browser window.

This second line indicates that the page to be displayed in the left window is the menu.htm file.
Every window has a name. Here we called it "left", but we could have specified any other name.
<frame name="left" src="menu02.htm">

</frameset>
The final line simply indicates that the frame structure declaration ends at this point.

<frame name="right" src="index02.htm">
Specifies that the Web page to be displayed in the right window is index02.htm, and that this window is called "right".

Click OK and save the page.

Since *Microsoft Front-Page Express* cannot be used to view a site composed of frames, we will use a browser to test it.

Thanks to the frame technique, the two *HTML* files are displayed in the same browser window, giving you the impression that there is only one file involved.

Links to other frames

Pages invoked by links are displayed in the window from which they were activated, unless otherwise specified.
In this case, the pages invoked from the right window will be displayed by default in that window; the pages invoked from links located in the left page will naturally be displayed in the left window. New pages invoked from links in the menu on the left must be displayed in the right window, otherwise there would be no point in having a menu displayed permanently.

1 In this example, the page on the beaches of Saint-Martin must be displayed when a user clicks on "Beaches" in the menu on the left.

Make sure that the two pages concerned have been opened in FrontPage Express.

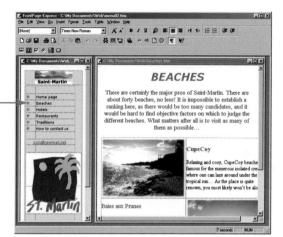

2 Select the words you want to use to create the link and then click Insert/Hyperlink.

Creating a link to a frame

Click the Open Pages tab and select the page you want. Finally, make sure you enter the name of the target window in the Target Frame field.

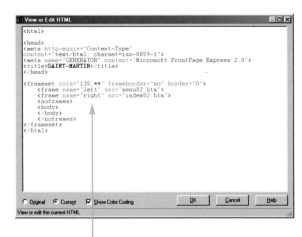

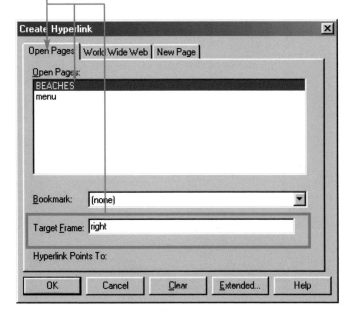

In this case, when the windows were created, the left page was named "left" and the right page was named "right".

The Target Frame field is used to specify the window (or frame) in which the page will be displayed when a user clicks on a link.

Selecting the target frame

There are names reserved for frames. The main ones are:

_self   The page is displayed in the same window as the link.

_blank   The page is displayed in a new window opened by the browser.

_top   The page is displayed in the entire browser screen. The windows disappear.

_parent   The page is displayed in the window from which it was called.

Tip

The reserved name "_top" is normally used to refer to an external Web site so that it will be displayed full-size in the browser window.

For example, let's create a new link from the word "HOTELS", which displays the page called "hotel.htm" full-size in the browser window.

Select the link and click Edit/Hyperlink.

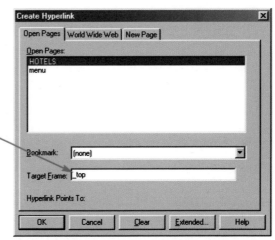

Select the page in question and enter the word "_top" in the Target Frame field.

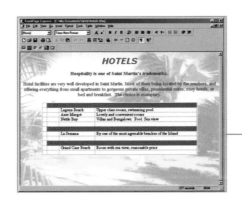

"_top" being one of the words reserved for frame names, the browser will understand that it should display the Web page full-size within the browser window, and thus make the frame structure invisible.

The menu on the left has disappeared.

Generic syntax

You have to bear in mind that a screen can only be divided in two ways: vertically or horizontally. If you want a more complex structure, you can use the Russian doll technique: the first window can be divided into two; each of the two resulting windows can then be divided into two..., and so on. The strategy is "divide and conquer".

We have used a specific example to show how to use the frame technique, and in particular how to create a site composed of two vertical windows. Let us now extend the principle to a site involving several windows.

To divide a window vertically, use the following HTML command:

<FRAMESET COLS='20%,80%'>

To divide a window horizontally, use the following HTML command:

<FRAMESET ROWS='20%,80%'>

The percentages given in the examples specify the size of each of the two windows and can be set as the Webmaster wishes. You may also wish to specify this size in pixels rather than in percentages.

A frame is actually a fully-fledged HTML page. Borders surround each frame you make, which may seem inelegant, but we will see that there are ways to get rid of this effect. Similarly, we can also get rid of the vertical scroll bars in the windows, which may otherwise spoil the look of the site. But watch out! A visitor will not be able to scroll through the text if you eliminate those bars... You must therefore consider carefully how much information you put in each of the frames you create.

General principle

Let us imagine a site structured as shown below. The page1.htm file contains the table of contents, accessible from all the other pages of the site; the page2.htm file contains a page of the site; and finally, page3.htm contains a second menu or other information that stays displayed.

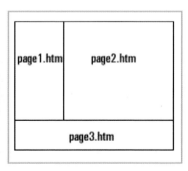

We will first divide the screen into two horizontal parts.

The corresponding HTML code is as follows (we'll replace the temporary second line in just a moment !):

```
<FRAMESET ROWS="80%,20%">
  <FRAME NAME="xxx"
SRC="yyy.htm">
  <FRAME NAME="window3"
SRC="page3.htm">
</FRAMESET>
```

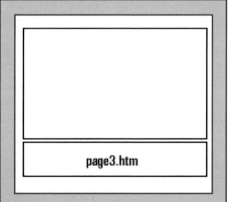

We will then divide the upper part into two vertical parts.

So we replace that second HTML line by :

```
<FRAMESET COLS="20%,80%">
  <FRAME NAME="window1"
SRC="page1.htm">
  <FRAME NAME="window2"
SRC="page2.htm">
</FRAMESET>
```

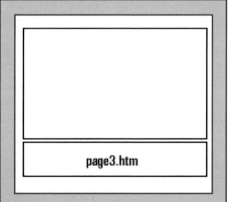

The HTML code

```
<FRAMESET ROWS="80%,20%">

 <FRAMESET COLS="20%,80%">
  <FRAME NAME="window1" SRC="page1.htm">
  <FRAME NAME="window2" SRC="page2.htm">
 </FRAMESET>

 <FRAME NAME="window3" SRC="page3.htm">

</FRAMESET>
```

When we put all that together, we get the structure we want.

A Web site structured in this way will contain at least four pages:

Page1.htm, Page2.htm, Page3.htm and the welcome page which describes the structure shown opposite (index02.htm, for example).

The <FRAMESET...> tag has several attributes:

BORDER	Used to specify the size of the borders surrounding the frames, expressed in terms of pixels. The value 0 indicates no border.
BORDERCOLOR	Used to specify the colour of all the borders of the frames, by name or hexadecimal value.
FRAMESPACING	Used to specify, in terms of pixels, the space between frames. The value zero indicates no space.

Example: <FRAMESET ROW="80%,20%" BORDER="0" FRAMESPACING="0">

The <FRAME...>tag has several attributes:

MARGINWIDTH	Used to specify the width of the left and right margins of the frame being created; the value must be expressed in pixels and can be 0.
MARGINHEIGHT	Used to specify the size of the upper and lower margins of the frame being created; the value must be expressed in pixels and can be 0.
FRAMEBORDER	Used to specify whether or not a frame is to have a border. Two values: YES or NO.
NORESIZE	Prevents the user from changing the size of the frames. By default, frames can be resized.
SCROLLING	Used to add a scroll bar to a frame or to remove it. Three possible values:
	YES: Means that the scroll bar will stay visible.
	NO: Means that the scroll bar will never be visible.
	AUTO: the browser will determine whether the scroll bar will be present.

Example: <FRAME NAME="window1" SRC="page1.htm" marginwidth="0" frameborder="NO" noresize scrolling="NO">

Incompatible browsers

The frame technique is useful for building a Web site. But you must remember that some older browsers cannot interpret these *HTML* commands. Frames appeared with version 3.0 of Netscape. Today, both Netscape and Internet Explorer can handle frames, but you have to consider what should happen if the site is visited by someone using an incompatible browser.

You can enter between the tags <noframes> and </noframes> instructions to the browser for handling such a situation.

The best solution is to link to the site's main page so that the visitor can see what your pages are all about.

Certain search engines have trouble referencing sites built using frames. To solve this problem, between the tags <noframes> and </noframes> you should enter a description of the site and links to its various pages.
The search engines can then proceed with referencing the pages without any difficulty.

1 Launch the welcome page of the site, which normally has no text, but which contains the structure of the frames.

2 Write a brief message telling visitors why they have got this page, and create a link to the site's main page.

3 In studying the *HTML* code, we see that the editor has added a <noframes> section automatically.

It is of course possible to design a more elaborate and better looking page ...

Counters

Creating a Web site is one thing; keeping track of visits to it is another.

You will naturally want to know how often your site is visited and by whom. Sometimes you may be surprised to find out that the site has been visited by people from abroad. In such a case, you should consider translating the site.

The Internet abounds in free services offering to provide you with statistics on site visits. In return, they will want you to put their company logo on your pages. Such a service is free only to non-commercial Web pages.

There are two types of services: counters, which simply count the number of visitors who have accessed your pages; and statistics, which provide a more precise account of site visits.

Freestuffcenter (http://www.freestuffcenter.com/sub/webmastertop.html) offers different kinds of counters for your Web pages.

The way to use these counters is explained clearly in each case.

Addresses of similar services offered through free sites are given on page 62.

Chapter 11

Forms

Introduction

A form is a Web page that visitors to your site can use to communicate with you, the site's creator. The visitor fills in the field with, for example, his or her surname, first name, etc., and then submits the form, usually to your e-mail address. When you check your e-mail therefore, you will find the forms sent from your site.

The form should be as simple and short as possible. Otherwise, you are likely to receive forms with fields left blank or incomplete. Similarly, you don't want to give the impression that you are prying into people's private lives by means of the questions included in your form.

A form can be sent in various ways. Some methods depend upon the server on which your Web pages are hosted, so you cannot always choose how the information will be submitted to you. The most common solution is to have the form sent to you via e-mail. The advantage of this method is that it will work regardless of where your Web site resides.

The mail you get may seem overwhelming at first. You will find, though, that you quickly become accustomed to it. Besides, this method is very simple to implement.

Form fields

Insert / Form fields

A form can be composed of several fields inserted into your Web pages by using *Insert/Form Field*.

Scrolling text box:
Used to enter one or more lines. Often it is used to allow the visitor to leave long comments.

One-line text box:
Used to enter a few words.

Check box:
Lets the visitor tick one or more options.

☐ Windows 95
☑ Windows 98

One-Line Text Box
Scrolling Text Box
Check Box
Radio Button
Drop-Down Menu
Push Button
Image

Radio button:
Lets the visitor choose one of several options.

● Boy
● Girl

Image:
Used to add an image to a form.

Push button:
Used to submit or clear the form.

SEND

Drop-down menu:
Used to permit a choice from a drop-down menu.

Saint-Martin ▾

Creating a form

It is best to put the fields of a form into the cells of a table. By doing this, you'll save yourself long hours of formatting, because with tables you can align the various form elements properly.

① Create the page that will contain the form. In this case, form.htm.

② Prepare a table of one row and one column, whose width is 500 pixels (Table/Insert Table).

③ Insert the first field of the form.

This is a text box.

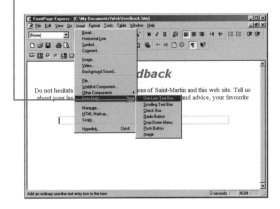

④ Place the cursor to the right of the field just inserted and create a table of 5 rows and 2 columns.

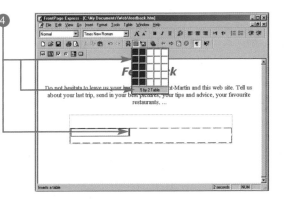

Formatting a table

1 You must now place the text box into the first cell of the table.

Use the mouse to select the text box.

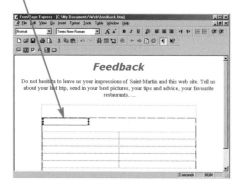

2 Click on Edit/Cut.

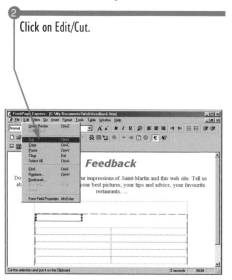

3 Using the mouse, place the cursor in the second column of the table and click on Edit/Paste.

4 The text box is now placed in the cell. Delete the extra spaces in the view above by pressing the Delete key on your keyboard.

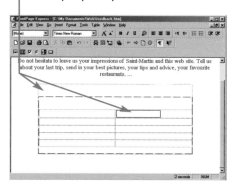

5 The form begins to take shape.

6 Now reduce the width of the first column to 100 pixels (Table/Cell Size).

Inserting fields

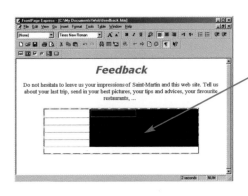

1 Set the size of the second column to 400 pixels (Table/Cell size).

The width of the first column being 100 pixels, and that of the second being 400, the table therefore is 500 pixels wide.

From this point, it is easy to complete the form by adding the other fields.

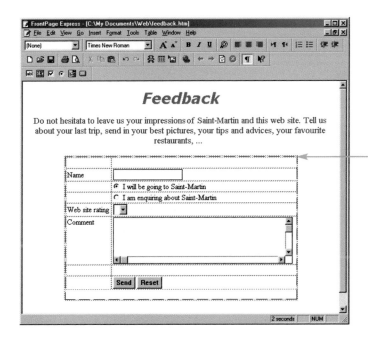

2 One by one add the various form fields (Insert/Form Field).

All the fields within the dotted box belong to the same form. So it is therefore possible to have several forms on one Web page.

3 Enter a heading in the right column and change the font style and size if necessary.

> Formatting is made much easier by using a table to create a form.

Properties of form fields

Once the form has been created, the properties of its fields can be edited so that default values are defined, a list of drop-down menus (if any) is established, a button for submitting and clearing the form is created, etc.

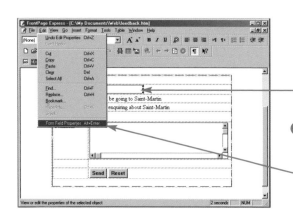

1 Select the first field of the form. Here we have a text box for a visitor's surname and first name.

2 Click Edit/Form Field Properties.

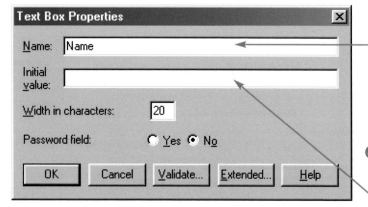

3 Enter a name in the Name field. This name must contain no spaces or unusual characters.

This name will help you keep track of the values reflected in your e-mail.

You can keep the default values, but it would make better sense to enter a pertinent name.

4 The Initial Value field lets you insert a default value into the form field, in case the visitor does not supply a value.

If you select "Yes" for "Password field", then the characters entered into the field by a user are replaced by asterisks (*) in display.

This comes in useful when confidential information is being entered.

Radio buttons

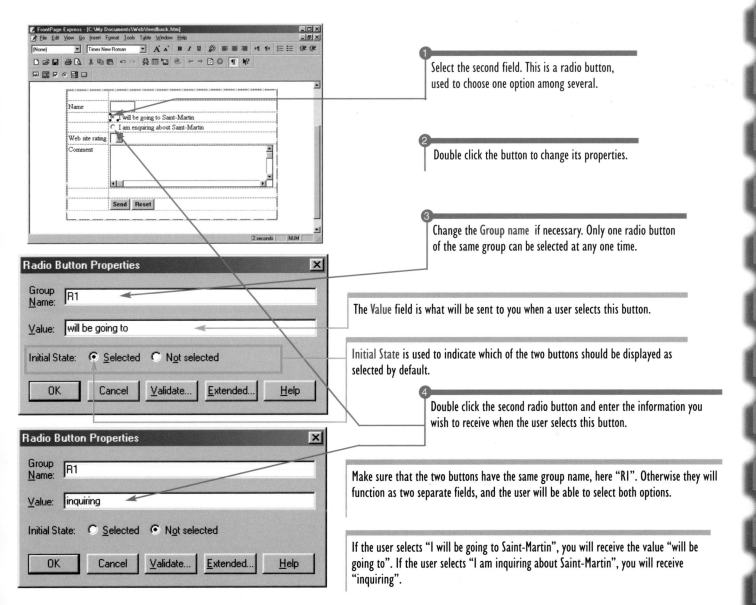

Select the second field. This is a radio button, used to choose one option among several.

Double click the button to change its properties.

Change the Group name if necessary. Only one radio button of the same group can be selected at any one time.

The Value field is what will be sent to you when a user selects this button.

Initial State is used to indicate which of the two buttons should be displayed as selected by default.

Double click the second radio button and enter the information you wish to receive when the user selects this button.

Make sure that the two buttons have the same group name, here "RI". Otherwise they will function as two separate fields, and the user will be able to select both options.

If the user selects "I will be going to Saint-Martin", you will receive the value "will be going to". If the user selects "I am inquiring about Saint-Martin", you will receive "inquiring".

Drop-down menu

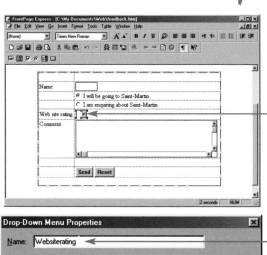

1 Select the fourth field. This is a drop-down menu visitors can use to let you know whether they like your Web site.

2 Double click on the field to change its properties.

3 Give a name to the field, taking care not to use any spaces or unusual characters.

4 Click the Add button to create the various choices that will appear in the menu.

You can change the value sent to you. The complete name is returned by default.

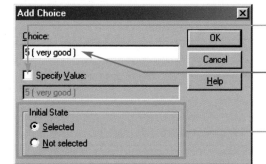

5 Enter the text you want to appear in the drop-down menu, and click OK.

Specify whether you want this choice to appear selected by default in the drop-down menu.

Drop-down menu (continued)

6

Proceed to create all the possible choices of the drop-down menu in the same way. Here, we will define three possible selections.

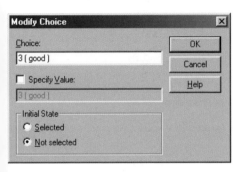

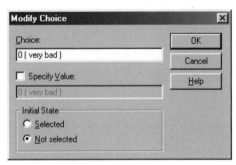

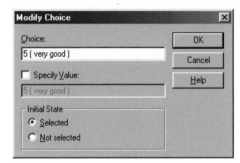

The choices that will appear in the drop-down menu now appear and can be edited.

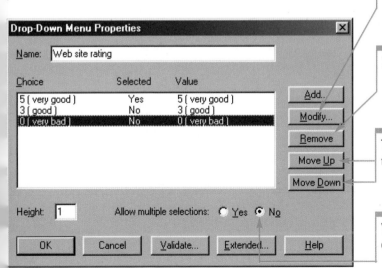

The **Modify** button can be used to modify the characteristics of those choices.

The **Remove** button is used to remove an entry.

The **Move Up** and **Move Down** buttons are used to define the order in which the choices are displayed in the drop-down menu.

You can allow multiple selections in the list. In this case, this feature is not enabled.

Text boxes

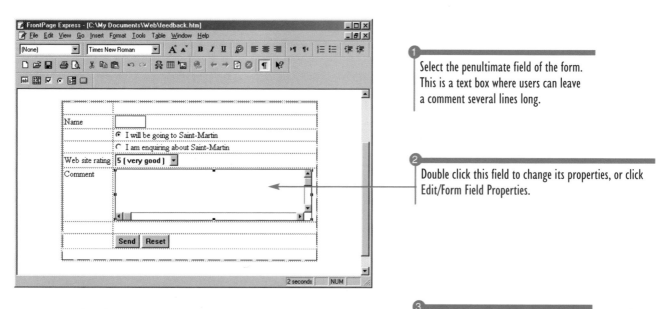

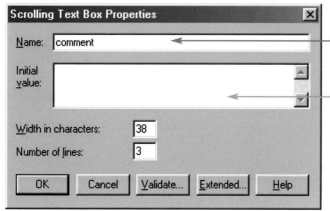

1 Select the penultimate field of the form. This is a text box where users can leave a comment several lines long.

2 Double click this field to change its properties, or click Edit/Form Field Properties.

3 Give a name to the field and click OK.

Here once again, you enter a default value that will be displayed for the user to adopt or modify.

The Send and Reset buttons

Every form must have at least one push-button, usually called *Submit or Send*, that users can press to submit the form. The e-mail address to which the form is to be sent is indicated in the properties of this button.

1 Change the properties of the two form buttons. One is used to submit the form; the other to clear all the values entered. Double click the Submit button.

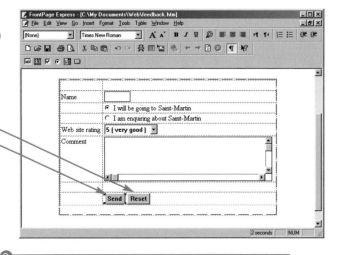

Push Button Properties

Name: **B1**

Value/Label: **Send**

Button type: ○ Normal   ● Submit   ○ Reset

[OK]   [Cancel]   [Extended...]   [Form...]   [Help]

2 The name "BI" of the Submit button is not really important, but you can change it nonetheless. Next, click on the Form button.

There are three types of preset buttons:

● "Normal" buttons are generally used to run scripts or other small Internet programs. We will not use such buttons in this book.

● "Submit" buttons are used exclusively to submit forms. The Submit button is used to specify the e-mail address to which the said form is to be sent. This button must be contained in the form without fail.

● "Reset" buttons are used exclusively with a form to clear what the user has entered in the fields. This button is optional, but useful nonetheless.

Button properties

Give your form a name; here "Contact".

Select Custom **ISAPI**, **NSAPI** or **CGI Script** and click the Settings button.

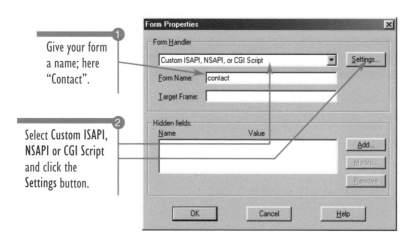

Enter the e-mail address to which the form is to be sent; here sxm@newmail.net. Remember to insert **mailto:** in front of the address.

Select the **POST** method.

Next enter a **text/plain** encoding type.

Click the last button, here called **Reset**, to change its properties.

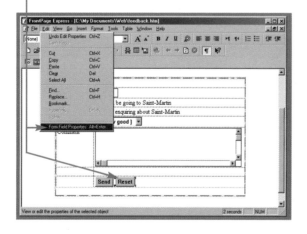

Click the **Reset** button to clear the form fields. Rename the button if necessary.

Testing the form

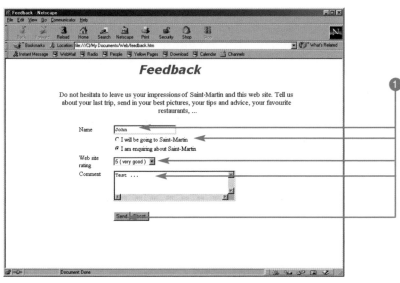

① Your form has now been created, and you should use your regular browser to test it. Connect to the Internet, fill in the fields and click Send.

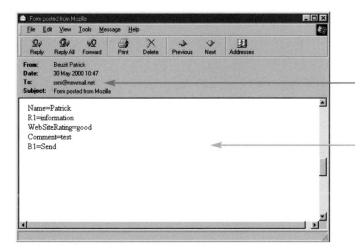

② Now get your e-mail from the e-mail address specified when the form was created: here sxm@newmail.net.

You will receive an e-mail in the form shown.

It is always best to give a clear and explicit name to the various form fields so as to make it easier to read the mail messages received.

Webbot components

The Webbot components, accessible from the Insert/Webbot menu, are small programs ready to be used to add new features to your Web pages. Similarly, the Scrolling Text option in the same Insert menu is used, as its name indicates, to have your text scroll without requiring a single line of programming.

The Web server that will host your Web site should support FrontPage extensions. In general, all Internet Service Providers offer hosting of Web pages. Ask yours whether FrontPage extensions are supported. If they are, you will be able to use the features of these components.

Some Webmasters prefer to use JavaScript, or to develop programming languages in Java, which have the advantage of working on any platform.

Be that as it may, Java and JavaScript lie beyond the scope of this book.

It is wise to avoid using proprietary techniques as much as possible.

Chapter 12

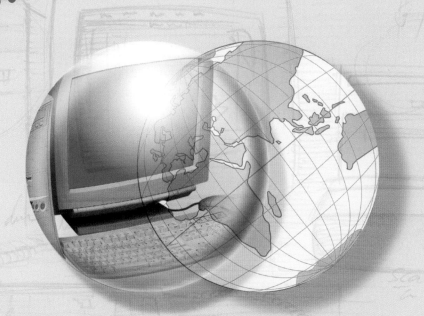

Publishing your site

Registering with a host

We have finally reached the last step, where you will publish your site on the Internet and make it available to all Web users. You will want to share your creation with the public and show off what you can do. You may be apprehensive that your site is incomplete or not as polished as it might have been. Don't worry; in any event, publishing your first site on the Internet will be quite an experience.

You now need to find a place on the Internet to publish your pages. Your first option is to use the disk space made available to you by your Internet Service Provider. Practically all providers offer space for publishing personal Web pages. Nevertheless you have to be careful to respect any restrictions imposed by your provider. For example, your site must not contain pornographic images or excerpts from documents used without the author's permission, etc.

Having your Website hosted by your Internet Service Provider is not your only option, however. You may prefer to use a free hosting service. Such services offer disk space, but will often require a small advertising banner to appear on your site when it is opened. Advertising is the price to pay for a few free megabytes of space. In addition to hosting your site, such services will often provide you with an e-mail address.

Finally, there are commercial hosts, who tend to serve mainly professionals, and will store your Web pages on their servers for a monthly fee. A large array of services are provided alongside the hosting service (e-mail, scripting, statistics, etc.).

Here is a list of some of the main hosts. You must respect the conditions of use of each of them.

http://www.dynahost.net	http://www.xoom.com
http://www.fortunecity.com	http://www.HostCompare.com
http://www.geocities.com	http://freeweblist.freeservers.com
http://www.webhostme.com	http://www.tripod.co.uk

Registering with a host (continued)

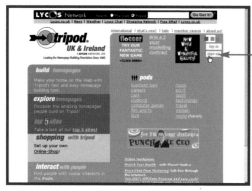

1 Click on sign-up.

2 A new screen will appear posting the conditions of use. Read it attentively and accept it at your discretion.

3 Choose a name, called Member name, that will be used for your Web site. At the same time, think of a sufficiently intricate password, but make sure you can remember it.

Next complete the personal details and confirm.

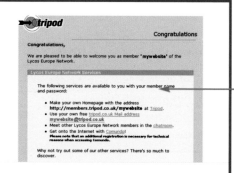

4 The system will now feed your identifier back to you and tell you your new Tripod e-mail address, which you can now use in communicating with your friends.

5 A e-mail will then be sent informing you that you are now registered.

We decided to register our Web site on Saint-Martin with *Tripod* (*www.tripod.co.uk*). This provider offers free non-commercial Web page hosting with 100 MB of disk space, provides an e-mail address and maintains a directory in which your site can be listed.

Closing the deal with *Tripod* took less than five minutes!

FTP client

The site is finished and you have found a server on which it can be hosted. The only thing left to do is to publish your masterpiece on the Internet, making it accessible to all from any corner of the world.

To this end, you will use an **FTP** client. This is a software application used to put on the Internet the various files used in creating your site: the **HTML** pages, images, sound files, etc...

There are many **FTP** clients. It is up to you, as **Webmaster**, to try out several and then to decide on the one that you think will best meet your needs. We opted for **Webdrive**.

Webdrive is an application under Windows 95/98 made available for free for 30 days. It is easy to use: it simulates a new hard disk in Windows Explorer. **Getting a Web** site online has never been easier.

All you have to do is to download **Webdrive**, which can be found on the Web at http://www.tucows.com.

On the same site, you can access other **FTP** clients as well as various **HTML** editors, so you can gauge better the power and limitations of **FrontPage Express**.

Some of the sites offering applications for creating Web pages:
http://www.tucows.com http://www.download.com http://www.shareware.com http://freeclutter.snap.com

Downloading an FTP client

1 Point your browser to www.tucows.com.

In the Quick Search box, enter the program name Webdrive.

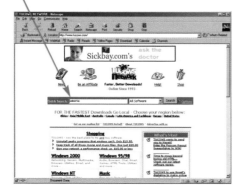

2 You have now found Webdrive. Read the description of the program, and then press Download now to download the file.

3 Select the continent where you live.

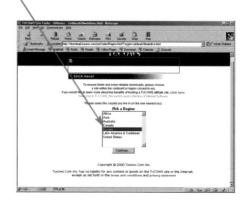

4 Select the country where you live, or if it is not listed, a neighbouring country.

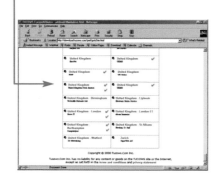

5 Click Save file and select the directory into which you want to copy the file.

6 The wdtrial.exe file is downloading....

Once you have downloaded the file, run *Windows Explorer*. Go to the directory in which you saved *wdtrial.exe* and double click on the file to install the program on your computer. Follow the instructions step by step. You are advised to accept the default values given by the installation program.

Publishing your site on the Internet

The site is ready to be published, but first check once more that it runs correctly. Check that all the links are working. Launch your browser and go through all the pages, because although a page may well be displayed properly while it's on your hard disk, this may not be the case once it is published on the Internet. If a link refers to a directory on your hard disk, C:\Windows, for instance, that directory will obviously not be found on the Internet. As we have emphasised, files must never refer directly to any of the drives on your computer.

Use several browsers to test your site, as it may not look the same on all browsers. Sometimes the differences can be astounding! So if you test your site with **Microsoft Internet Explorer** and its rival, **Netscape Navigator**, you will able to gauge the differences and make corrections accordingly. Reread the pages of your site carefully. You must take particular care with spelling and grammar. Finally, consider the size of your site (in kilobytes). Many free servers limit the amount of disk space available. To know the size of your files and images, right-click on the folder that holds your site and select 'Properties' in the context menu. The total size of the files and folders will be shown in megabytes.

1

In Windows, run WebDrive from Start/Programs/WebDrive. Double click the Make New Connection Icon.

2

Enter a name for the connection and the address of the FTP server to which you want to connect.

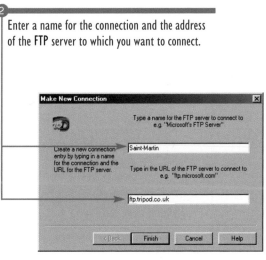

Your host must communicate the address of the FTP server to the Internet Service Provider.

Publishing your site on the Internet (continued) ...

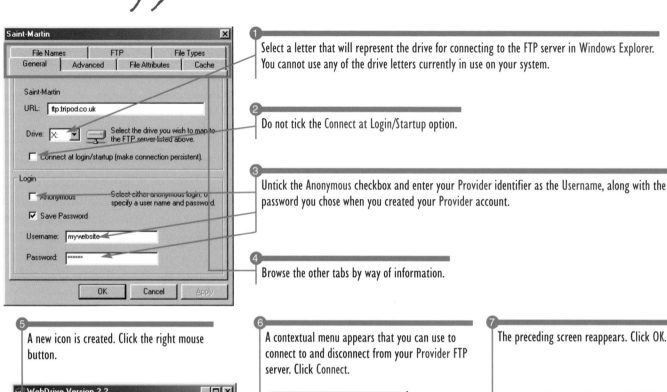

1 Select a letter that will represent the drive for connecting to the FTP server in Windows Explorer. You cannot use any of the drive letters currently in use on your system.

2 Do not tick the Connect at Login/Startup option.

3 Untick the Anonymous checkbox and enter your Provider identifier as the Username, along with the password you chose when you created your Provider account.

4 Browse the other tabs by way of information.

5 A new icon is created. Click the right mouse button.

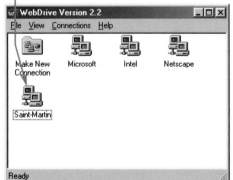

6 A contextual menu appears that you can use to connect to and disconnect from your Provider FTP server. Click Connect.

7 The preceding screen reappears. Click OK.

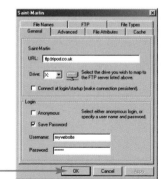

Publishing your site on the Internet (continued)

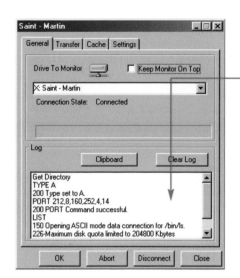

8 The logon parameters for the server are displayed in the control window. Click OK.

9 You are finally connected to your Provider FTP server.

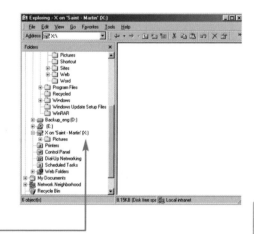

10 Launch Windows Explorer.

11 A new drive appears in Windows Explorer, i.e. X.
This virtual drive is comparable to any other hard disk or disk drive.

12 Drive X: is the Tripod disk on which you can copy your Web pages. This is not a local disk. It is located several kilometres or even hundreds or thousands of kilometres away from your house.

Nothing and no one can prevent you from using this disk space as any other hard disk. You can use it to store your files, programs, etc. Just remember that they will be accessible from the Internet.

You can use this disk in the same way as you use your usual hard disk. Copy your files by dragging them to X: We will use the *copy / paste* method.

Publishing your site on the Internet (conclusion)

1 Go to your Web site's working directory and select all the files and subdirectories that it contains.

Next, click **Edit / Copy** to copy this selection.

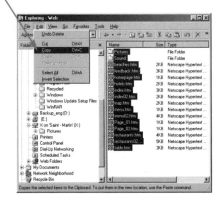

2 Now go to your x: drive and paste the files by clicking **Edit / Paste**.

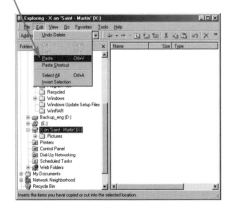

3 The file transfer then begins automatically. The files and subdirectories will be copied onto the Provider site. Only the relatively slow transfer time gives any hint that you are working with a remote hard disk.

4 Once the file transfer has been completed, the files appear on the hard disk of the **Provider FTP** server.

5 Note the icon located in the lower right-hand corner of your monitor. This is the **Webdrive** icon. Double click on it.

6 Click **Disconnect** to disconnect from the Provider server.

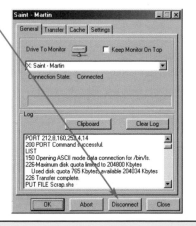

Good news... Your site can now be seen from anywhere in the world.

Search engines

Very often, you access a **Web** site for the first time by using a **search engine**. Remember that a search engine is a site equipped to permit searching for other sites using keywords chosen by the Net user. A well indexed site therefore has the best chance of being visited.

There are two types of **search engines**: search engines proper and **directories**. Querying a **search engine** involves entering one or more keywords. The engine then returns a list of sites matching the search criteria.

Directories on the other hand classify sites under headings, rather like the directories or sub-directories on your hard disk. You therefore use a directory by browsing the headings to a greater and greater depth until you find the site you want.

International search engines and directories...	
http://www.alltheweb.com	http://www.hotbot.com
http://www.altavista.com	http://www.infoseek.com
	http://www.lifestyle.co.uk
altavista: SEARCH	http://www.lycos.com
http://www.askjeeves.com	http://searchenginewatch.com
http://www.excite.com	http://www.sitexplorer.com
http://www.excite.co.uk	http://www.webcrawler.com
	http://www.yahoo.com
eXcite.	http://www.yahoo.co.uk

Getting your site indexed

Simply notifying a search engine that a site exists can have disappointing results. In the best cases, the site will be cited somewhere in the first twenty pages returned by the engine. Bearing in mind that Net surfers hardly ever look beyond the second page... you can see that this approach could mean that your site will never be found!

There is no guarantee your site will be found, but you can improve the odds by embedding certain *HTML* commands as you build it. Many search engines use these commands for indexing. That's why it's so important not to forget this step.

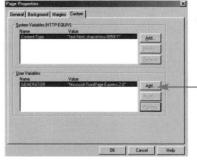

1 On the FrontPage Express menu File/Page Properties, click the Custom tab. Click the Add button found inside the User Variables box.

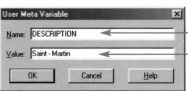

2 In the Name field, enter "DESCRIPTION" and in the Value field provide a description of your site.

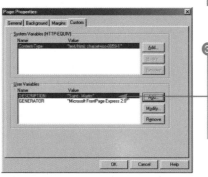

3 For purposes of verification, the description is displayed in the window.

The choice of keywords can become complicated for the Webmaster but you should follow these three basic rules:

Don't use words that are already used in the pages of the site.

Think through carefully the use of common keywords (for example, 'tourism'). Entering "tourism" when using a search engine will generate a huge list of sites, but you should still include it because it could be used with other words as part of an advanced search (for example, tourism+africa).

Put yourself in the place of an Internet user who is searching for the exact contents of your Web site.

The descriptive text is what search engines use to present the site to Web surfers. You should therefore take special care in wording that text. It must clearly and explicitly summarize the content of your site. Make a description for each page. The length of the descriptive text depends on the search engine being used, more than anything else. As a general rule, this text can contain from 50 to 200 words, but it is best to keep it to 50.

Getting your site indexed (continued)

Next you need to list the keywords relating to your site. Choose about fifty reasonably relevant words.

The directories often show only the descriptive text and keywords, so it is important to use keywords that are meaningful and truly appropriate to your site. Very commonly used words (such as sex, money, free, etc.) should be avoided. Likewise, very general words (such as Internet, multimedia, etc.) are of small benefit.

Repeating the same word several times is a trick that search engines easily recognize. You will probably incur a penalty for doing that. Slightly varying the spelling of a particular word is a better alternative.

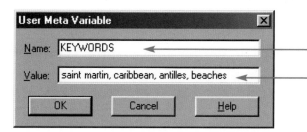

Add a second variable: "KEYWORDS". Enter a number of keywords, separated by commas and using lower-case letters. It is better to use singular instead of plural (for example, "ocean" rather than "oceans").

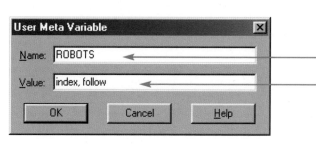

Another variable that enhances indexing is "ROBOTS" when it contains the values, Follow and Index. This tells the search engine to index the page and also to trace the links made from that page.
The values Nofollow or Noindex make it impossible to index the page or to trace its links.

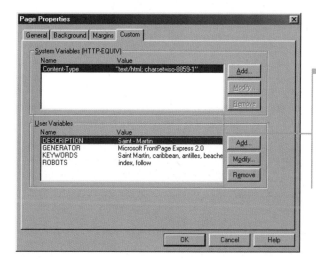

The different User variables allow you to optimise the way a particular search engine handles your site. Nevertheless, nothing can guarantee that your site will be found in the first several pages returned by a search engine.

Improving your pages

The title of each page (*File/Page Properties* - see chapter 3) must be clear and concise. If possible the first word should start with one of the first letters of the alphabet (**directories** list sites in alphabetical order). Try to include some of the most important keywords in the title.

Avoid boastful titles ("The Best Web Sites", "Everything You Need to Know About...", etc.). Avoid special characters in the title description, because some search engines do not handle them well. Finally, do not use all capitals, as that practice is looked down on.

You as the **Webmaster** should make sure that there is a distinctive title for every page on your site.

Some search engines use the first few sentences on a site for the purpose of indexing the site.

The best thing to do is to design your site in such a way that the first page starts with a very explicit sentence using a number of meaningful keywords. In our Saint-Martin site, we start with: "Orient Bay, Long Bay, Oyster Pond, Maho Beach... fabulous, sun-drenched, sandy beaches, with limpid blue waters, the lapping of the waves, the fragrance of the bracing brine-soaked wind..."

Obviously, it would not be helpful to use an image as a title; hence the need to caption each image. Some search engines use image captions for indexing purposes.

Avoid putting silly or uninteresting comments as the text associated whith your images (for example, title.gif or welcome.jpg).

Finally, as the months go by and you continue to work on your site, avoid eliminating pages if you can, because they may have been indexed by one search engine or another. Deleting them would amount to creating broken links, and visitors will be discouraged. It is better to design a page that will refer the **Web** user to the revised site.

A site built with frames can be problematic for most search engines. So, between <noframes>... </noframes>, you should enter a precise description of the site together with the links to other pages. The search engines can then proceed with indexing.

Registering the site

Indexing a site is theoretically easy, but how it is done depends on the search engine used, i.e. whether it is a search engine proper or a directory.

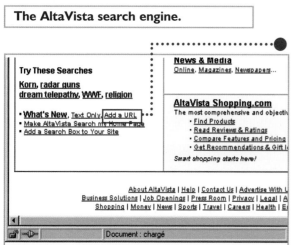

The AltaVista search engine.

In the case of a search engine, you simply have to find a link such as "Add a site" or "Add a URL" on its homepage. Look carefully because such links often get lost in the mass of information presented there. Once you have clicked on this link, you just have to enter the URL of your site and possibly an e-mail address where you can be contacted.

The search engines index pages, not sites, so they may refer you to several pages belonging to the same site. Hence a Net user may reach your site at some page other than the main page. Consequently, it is crucial to include on each page a link that refers back to the homepage.

Registering with a directory involves having to determine the heading under which your site should be listed. You should therefore go to that heading, as if you were conducting a search. Once you have determined the category or subcategory, just click on a link such as "Add a site" and then answer the questions asked; these are often more numerous than those asked by search engines. Directories index sites, so you should not request the indexing of several pages of the same site.

Several days or even weeks may go by between the time when the site is submitted to the search engine and when it is actually indexed... Just be patient and don't yield to the temptation of repeating the procedure.

Finally, it is up to you as the Webmaster to keep your site up to date and have search engines and directories index it regularly.

http://www.addme.com   http://www.addengine.com

Registering with Yahoo

Go to the heading that corresponds best to the subject matter of your Web site. Click Suggest a site.

First read the introductory text and notices.

Now complete the fields one by one.

We are going to register our tourism site with Yahoo (*http://www.yahoo.com*).

Registering with a search engine is easier, so we won't cover that here. All you have to do is provide the *URL* of the site.

The site is registered with the directory in less than five minutes. But you will have to wait several days or weeks before it is actually taken into account.

Bear in mind that Yahoo reserves the right to refuse a site.

Indexing robots

Registering a site with a directory or a search engine is not complicated in itself. It will take about ten minutes at most. If you want to register with several engines, on the other hand, you will have to spend a lot more time.

One solution is to make use of the services (free in the case of personal pages) that will register your site with several search engines at one go.

A wide selection of such services is given in the list of free sites on page 62.

Euro Submit
(http://www.eurosubmit.com/)
is one of these Web sites that
will index your work.

Enter the characteristics of the site to be indexed.
Indexer will then go through various search engines.

Some search engines visit a site only once. So you should have the site re-indexed on a regular basis.

Other indispensable services

Syntax checker

One might think that a Web site built using an HTML editor such as Microsoft FrontPage Express would be error-free. To make sure that this is the case, why not try one of the syntax checkers? These services, which are just as numerous as indexing services, will thoroughly check a Web site. Of course, you can test a Web site only after you've put it on the Internet, and not when it is simply stored on your computer. Several HTML editors, e.g. HoTMetaL Pro, will check your HTML locally.

URL rerouting

These services enable you to choose the URL of your Web site. Rather than have a site with an address that includes the name of your Internet Service Provider, you can choose a more discreet name such as http://come.to/alias or http://welcome.to/alias, where "alias" is a name of your choosing.

Counters

As we have already seen, counters keep track of how many users visit your Web site.

CGI Script, JavaScript, Java, etc.

A number of services offer small programs that can be used directly in a Web site. A knowledge of programming languages and HTML is recommended nonetheless.

E-mail rerouting

These services provide you with a new e-mail address. Any message sent to that address will be automatically rerouted to the one made available by your Internet Service Provider, for example.

Rather than giving a list of such services, which is bound to become obsolete in a few months, it is better to give the URL of Web sites that can be used to index them. These are called "portals", probably because they constitute a gateway to the Internet. Please refer to the free sites (page 62) which are teeming with useful addresses for Webmasters.

Chapter 13

Appendices

Help On-line

Here are a few addresses that will provide more in-depth information on how to design Web sites.

http://www.kevjudge.co.uk

This site explains how to create a personal Web site and provides useful tools and information for the Webmaster.

http://members.aol.com/teachemath/class.htm

This site explains how to build a personal Web site step by step.

http://www.simplebuilder.net

A guide on how to develop a site in HTML, on forms and on frames.

http://webmaster.tophosts.com

One of the largest resources for creating personal Web pages. Introduction to JavaScript.

http://www.htmlgoodies.earthweb.com

Another highly popular site on HTML and Web languages.

http://bignosebird.com

More than 250 tutorials, references and other resources on creating Web pages.

http://www.wsabstract.com/webresource/html.htm

List of resources on HTML-related sites.

http://reallybig.com/default.shtml

A gigantic portal on how to create HTML pages (clipart, CGI, counters, Java, etc).

Keyboard shortcuts

The main functions of the FrontPage Express editor can be accessed by means of keyboard shortcuts. You will save precious time as you get used to these shortcuts.

CTRL+N	New page
CTRL+O	Open a new page
CTRL+S	Save a page
CTRL+P	Print
CTRL+A	Select All
CTRL+F	Find
CTRL+H	Replace
CTRL+K	Create a hypertext link
CTRL+C	Copy
CTRL+X	Cut
CTRL+V	Paste
CTRL+B	Bold
CTRL+I	Italic
CTRL+U	Underline
CTRL+Z	Cancel
CTRL+Y	Restore
CTRL+M	Right indent
CTRL+SHIFT+M	Left indent
ALT+ENTER	Selected object properties

Glossary

Animated GIF:	Animated image in GIF format.
Bookmark:	Name that identifies a precise location in a document.
Clipart:	Drawing, logo or other graphic image.
Download:	Retrieving or transferring a file from another computer to your own.
Extension:	The last three characters of a file-name (after the dot), which indicate the type of file.
Freeware:	Software given away for free.
FTP:	File Transfer Protocol.
GIF:	Graphic Interchange Format used to store images to be displayed on a Web page. Ideal for images containing many areas of solid colour.
Homepage:	Welcome page of a Web site.
HTML:	Hyper Text Markup Language used to create pages on the Internet.
HTML editor:	Software used to design Web pages.
Indexing:	A method used to include a Web site in the listing of a search engine.
Internet:	The vast system of computer networks that are linked together all around the world.
ISP:	Internet Service Provider.
Java, JavaScript:	Multi-platform programming languages recognised by all the latest browsers, enabling programmers to enhance the basic effects of HTML.
JPEG:	Joint Photographic Expert Group used to store images to be displayed on a Web page. Ideal for complex pictures, eg. photos, paintings.
Login:	Identifier (user name) used by a surfer to identify him/herself when accessing a server.
Offline:	Using your computer without being connected to the Internet.
Online:	Using your computer while connected to the Internet.
Password:	A word or words used to authenticate your identity when connecting to a server.
Pixel:	Short for picture element, the smallest single point that can be displayed on a screen.
Search engine:	Database used to search for documents on the Web.
Server:	Computer connected to the Internet and holding material accessible to other computers.
Shareware:	Software available free for a trial period, after which a fee is payable if you decide to use it.
Spreadsheet:	Software for creating tables and carrying out automatic calculations.
Tag:	HTML instruction code.
URL:	Uniform Resource Locator. Address of a Web site.
Webmaster:	Person who manages a Web site.
Web site:	Set of Web pages.
World Wide Web (Web, W3, WWW):	Probably the best known Internet service, where documents can be consulted using a browser. Uses hypertext technology.
Zip:	A file compression format.

INDEX

INDEX

INDEX